MANAGEMENT ☰SUCCESSION☰

From the Owner-Founder to the Professional President

Maryam Tashakori

PRAEGER

PRAEGER SPECIAL STUDIES • PRAEGER SCIENTIFIC

Library of Congress Cataloging in Publication Data

Tashakori, Maryam.
　Management succession.

　Bibliography:　p.
　1.　Executives--United States--Recruiting.
2.　Entrepreneur.　3.　Organizational change.
I.　Title.
HF5500.3.U54T38　　　　658.4'0711　　　80-13722
ISBN 0-03-047076-5

Published in 1980 by Praeger Publishers
CBS Educational and Professional Publishing
A Division of CBS, Inc.
521 Fifth Avenue, New York, New York 10017 U.S.A.

© 1980 by Maryam Tashakori

0123456789　038　987654321

Printed in the United States of America

ACKNOWLEDGMENTS

This book owes its existence to the cooperation of more than seventy individuals from more than thirty organizations. I would particularly like to thank the members of the four firms in which I conducted in-depth field work. I greatly appreciate their generosity in lending their time and sharing with me information about their firms and providing their candid opinions.

I would like to thank Professors Joseph L. Bower, Alfred D. Chandler, Jr., and John J. Gabarro of Harvard Business School for the advice and assistance they have provided me throughout all phases of this research. I am especially grateful to Professor Bower for the guidance he gave me during my thesis work and also throughout my doctoral studies at Harvard Business School.

I am grateful to my parents, Seifollah and Mahin Tashakori, for the opportunity and encouragement they have provided me to pursue higher education. This book is dedicated to my husband, David C. Wehe, with my gratitude for his sustained understanding and support.

CONTENTS

LIST OF FIGURES AND TABLES

MANAGEMENT SUCCESSION

1

INTRODUCTION

The purpose of this study is to examine the succession of owner-founders by professional managers as company presidents. The selection process leading to the choice of this management problem is presented below, with the assumption that insight into the evolution of the research topic will enable the reader to better understand the end product of a process involving months of work.

EVOLUTION OF THE RESEARCH TOPIC

The management problem that was initially chosen for study was the employment of outside managers in family businesses. Family businesses were defined as enterprises where the majority of stock was held by one family and where the firm's founder or one of his relatives served as president.* Outside managers were defined as managers who were *not* related to the owner-founder.

As the result of interviews with venture capitalists, it became evident that employment of outside managers encompassed two distinct situations. In the first situation, the owner-founder or a family member served as president, and outside managers were employed to serve as the firm's executives. In the second situation, an outside manager was appointed to

---

*The masculine pronoun is being used for succinctness and is intended to refer to both females and males.

1

replace the owner-founder or a family member as president. Each situation was broad enough to warrant an individual study. The decision was made to focus on the employment of an outside manager as president and to leave the other situation for a separate study.

Further literature review and interviews with venture capitalists and other managers regarding the replacement of family members as president by outside managers resulted in additional modification of the research focus. Simon A. Hershon's study, in particular, points out that there are important differences between replacement of the owner-founder and the replacement of second-generation or later presidents.[1] Other authors such as Zaleznik and Kets de Vries, in *Power and the Corporate Mind*, and Anne Jardim, in *The First Henry Ford: A Study in Personality and Business Leadership*, confirmed the unique nature of the process of replacing the owner-founder as president.[2] On the basis of these studies and interview data, it was decided to narrow the research focus further to situations where the owner-founder was replaced as president by an outside manager (Figure 1). Furthermore, it followed that the companies selected for study were managed by the owner-founder before the outside president was appointed. The ownership criterion—that the firm should be majority-owned by the owner-founder and his family—was discarded so that the findings could be generalized more readily. The term owner-founder, consequently, does not necessarily imply majority ownership by the founder or his family at the time of the study, although this may have been the case early in the organization's history.

The study specifically focuses on the three following questions: Why is the president appointed and what is the appointment process? How is the succession process viewed by the owner-founder, the new president, the executives, and the board of directors? What differentiates successful transitions from unsuccessful ones?

Two prior studies in particular have attested to the importance of the transition from owner-founder to outside president. Steinmetz, Kline, and Stegall, in *Managing the Small Business*, identified succession of the owner-founder as being crucial to the firm's survival:

> "Of all the causes of failure, particularly among small companies, the lack of early and adequate attention to the problem of management succession is far and away the most important."[3]

In his study of close to a hundred of the largest U.S. industrial firms, Alfred D. Chandler stated:

> The broad survey of American industrial companies also reinforces a point suggested in the case studies on General Motors and Sears, Roebuck as well as DuPont. This is that nothing is more crucial to the later history

FIGURE 1

Evolution of Research Topic

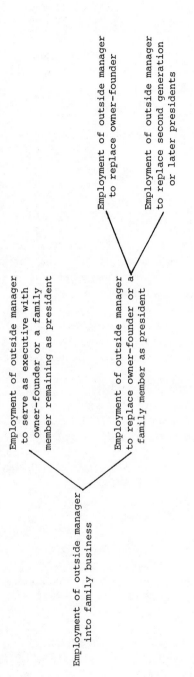

Source: Contructed by the author.

3

of the firm than the way in which its founders or their families make their terms with the administrative imperatives of large-scale enterprise.[4]

The objective of this study investigates one method used by firms to meet the change in the firm's management requirement—the appointment of an outside president.

LITERATURE REVIEW

Early in the course of research, it became evident that the replacement of the owner-founder by an outside president often involved two concurrent transitions for the organization. The first was the succession from one leader to another leader. The second was a transition from an entrepreneurial style of management to a professional style of management (Figure 2).[5] The large majority of owner-founders had entrepreneurial styles, whereas the outside managers, brought in to replace the owner-founder, usually had professional management styles. Consequently, the transition in the majority of cases was a diagonal one rather than a horizontal one. In his study of succession in family businesses, Hershon identified a similar occurrence in the transition from the owner-founder to his son or another relative. The familial and organizational changes took place concurrently.

Due to the change in management style inherent in most successions, the research problem was seen as merging two lines of inquiry: research on management succession and research on stages of development of the firm. Neither of these bodies of literature, however, specifically investigated the management issue examined in this study.

Many books, particularly those on small business management or the psychology of entrepreneurs, refer briefly to management succession; however, few have focused on the succession of the organization's president. A notable exception is C. Roland Christensen's *Management Succession in Small and Growing Enterprises*.[6] In this study, Christensen reported on interviews he had conducted with more than a hundred top managers in seeking to answer this question posed by the top manager of small businesses: "How can I help insure my company's survival by making certain that replacement management will be available when I go out of the picture?" Christensen's study discussed the pros and cons of the alternative preparations for succession: the use of interim management, appointment of a "crown prince," or the development of the company's management team. He also pointed out the common characteristics of enterprises that have successfully dealt with management succession.

Hershon studied management succession from one family generation to the next. He identified three successive "patterns of organizational charac-

FIGURE 2

Transitions Inherent in the Succession

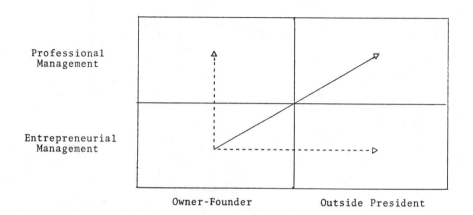

Source: Constructed by the author.

teristics" through which most firms pass: close supervision, collaborative management, and collective management. His major finding as described above was that the transition from one pattern of management to another often occurred with succession from one generation to another (Figure 3).

Although the present study also deals with management succession, its focus is different from those of Christensen and Hershon. Hershon examined replacement of the owner-founder by family members, whereas this study investigates succession by presidents who are not relatives. While Christensen's research took in the subject of replacing the owner-founder as well as other classes of president, this study deals exclusively with the replacement of owner-founders. Furthermore, Christensen focused on what managers can do to prepare for succession. This study aims to describe the events that take place before the president is appointed (i.e., the process of appointment), as well as the problems that arise after the new president enters the firm. The second important difference between the present study and those of Christensen and Hershon is in the research methodology. Whereas those authors opted for breadth, Christensen having conducted interviews at more than one hundred firms and Hershon at more than thirty, the study at hand has opted for depth through a detailed examination of the succession at four firms.

FIGURE 3
Relative Frequency of Sample Firm Experience

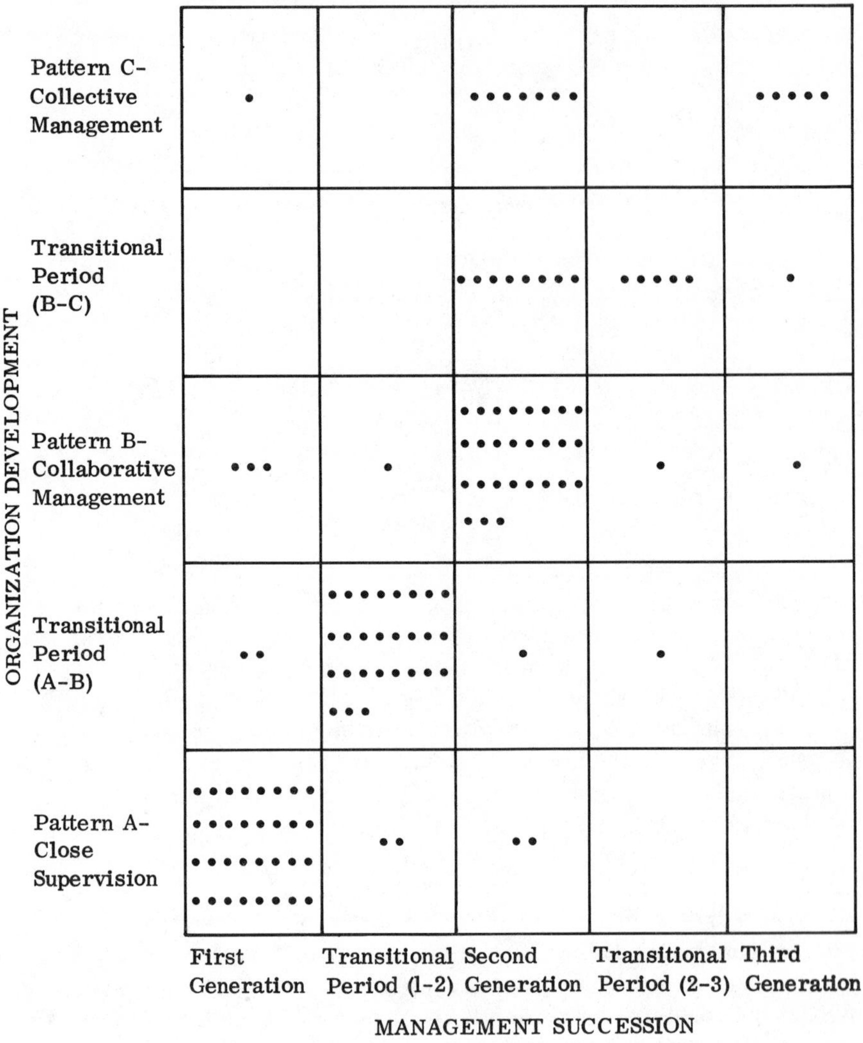

Source: Simon A. Hershon, "The Problems of Management Succession in Family Businesses (D.B.A. dissertation, Harvard University, Graduate School of Business Administration, 1975).

The second type of literature relevant to the present study was that dealing with the company's stages of development. The changes undergone in this progress have been a matter of interest to both businessmen and authors. In *Strategy and Structure*, Chandler identified five phases of development in the firm's structure, caused by changes in the firm's strategy, for the purpose of keeping resources effectively employed.[7] Bruce R. Scott's model of growth, however, was based on three stages as opposed to Chandler's five. Scott identified each stage by a cluster of managerial characteristics, one of which was the company's structure.[8]

Lippit and Schmidt identified three stages of organization development: birth, youth, and maturity. They define each stage by the crises that the company must deal with at that point.[9] Greiner characterized the firm's development as a series of evolutions, that is to say, periods of prolonged growth with little disruption, followed by revolutions, turbulent times with serious upheaval of management practices. He defined each evolutionary period by its possession of a dominant style that had been the solution to the past revolution and that became the cause of the next revolution as the organization grew in age and size.[10] Steinmetz delineated four stages of organizational growth. Like Greiner, he described each stage in terms of the dominant problems facing the firm and the management style used during that stage. Unlike the other authors, he further delineated each stage by determining the firm's size in specific numbers of employees and size of asset.[11]

Though all of the authors cited dealt with the development of the firm, all except Chandler focused on identifying stages of development rather than on discussing how the transition occurs. Chandler, however, concentrated on the transition in the firm's structure from a functional to a divisional structure. The paucity of research that focuses on the transition from owner-founder to outside president served as further justification to undertake the present study.

RESEARCH METHODOLOGY

An exploratory research methodology was used in this study. The researcher first gathered the data and then attempted to describe and explain them, by using already existing conceptual frameworks or theories and generating new ones. This approach differs considerably from the approach used by some researchers, of first selecting or formulating hypotheses or theories and then gathering data to test their validity.

The exploratory methodology was selected as being appropriate for studying succession from owner-founder to outside president for two reasons. Because of the sparsity of existing material regarding this topic, most theories selected or formulated prior to the field work would have had a high chance of being inappropriate to the problem under study. This would have resulted in forcing the data to fit the theory. Secondly, premature focus on testing particular hypotheses or theories could have directed the researcher's attention away from the important characteristics of the succession process and the most relevant explanations for the process. Consequently, because of the insufficient amount of knowledge regarding the topic at the time of the research, it was concluded that an exploratory methodology would be more appropriate than formulation and testing of hypotheses.

Stages of Research

This research was done in two stages. The objective of the first stage was to develop an understanding of the major problems and occurrences during the succession process. An extensive review of the literature and examination of relevant cases at Intercollegiate Case Clearing House was conducted. This was followed by interviews with experts who had participated in several successions. This group was composed of venture capitalists, lawyers, consultants, owner-founders, and presidents who had replaced the owner-founder. During this phase of the investigation, the scope of the topic was defined and narrowed in the manner described above.

The second stage involved in-depth field work at four companies where an outside president had been brought in to replace the owner-founder. On the basis of our findings in the first stage of the research, two variables were determined important to obtaining a representative sample: management complexity and existence or lack of a crisis before the president's appointment. Management complexity was broken down into high and low categories. Consequently, the sample design formed a two-by-two matrix as illustrated in Figure 4.

High and low complexities were defined as shown in Table 1. The literature review and the interview data indicated that high complexity tended to reduce the problems involved in the changeover to outside presidents. Greater complexity brought about an increase in the number of employees who were not related to the owner-founder. Secondly, higher complexity along the dimensions of size, products, and market forced the owner-founder to delegate decision making to the president. Lastly, it was thought that it would be more likely for owner-founders of high technology firms to be more interested in research than in administration and so more prone to delegating to the new president.

Crisis was identified as an important variable for two reasons. A crisis, whether brought on by poor financial results or deterioration in the relationship between the owner-founder and his executives would point out the

FIGURE 4
Sample Design

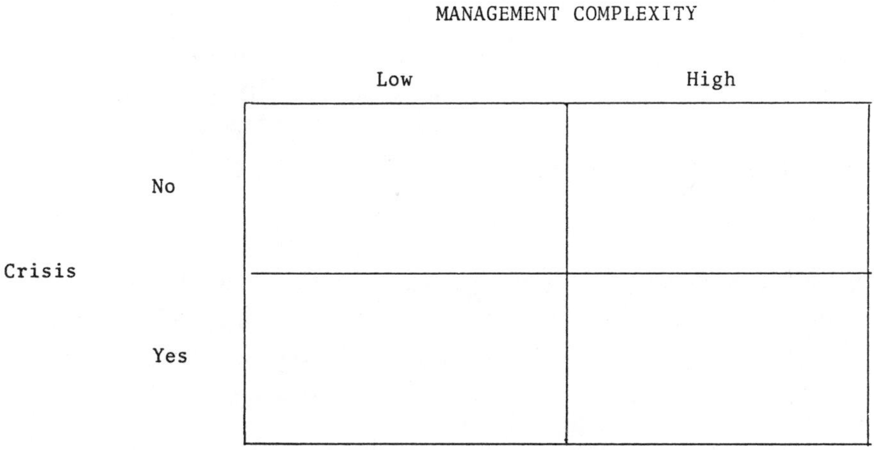

MANAGEMENT COMPLEXITY

	Low	High
No		
Yes		

Crisis

Source: Compiled by the author.

inadequacy of the owner-founder's management and the need for a new president. This would result in more support by the board and employees for a new president. Based on the data gathered in the first stage of research, it was expected that the new president in a company with no crisis and low complexity would have the most problems. The new president in a high complexity firm, where there was a crisis prior to his appointment, would have the easiest transition.

The four sites at which in-depth field work was conducted represent the four categories of the sample design (Figure 5). Design Associates* is an industrial design firm. Metal Manufacturing Company manufactures metal parts according to customer specifications. Home Mortgages is a mortgage banking company concentrating on single-family loans. Control Systems Inc. designs and manufactures measuring instruments used in process control systems. The companies represent service and manufacturing industries, low and high technology industries, and firms with low and high capital require-

---

*The names of all of the companies, their size and financial data, as well as the names of all of the participants in the study, have been changed. In some cases the industries in which the firms operate have also been changed.

TABLE 1
Definition of Management Complexity*

Item	Low Complexity	High Complexity
Product		
Number of products	Few	Several
Similarity of product lines	Related, same Concept	Diverse, multiple concepts
Similarity of manufacturing methods	High	Low
Market		
Number of channels of distribution	Few similar ones	Many diverse ones
Number of customer segments	Few	Many different ones
Geographic distribution	Regional or national	International
Technology		
Technical content of product	Very low, simple	Complicated and technical
Rate of scientific innovation inherent in products	Slow	Fast
Size		
Number of employees	Less than 50	Greater than 50

*This definition of complexity draws on Chandler's and Clifford's studies.

ments. Their sales range from approximately $4 million to over $150 million. They are dispersed geographically across the United States. Finally, the sample includes both successful and unsuccessful successions.

Field Work at Four Sites

The field work took place over a period of 17 months. The bulk of the field work consisted of interviews with the owner-founders, the new presidents, the top executives, and key board members. The interviews were supplemented by observation of meetings and other interaction among executives, whenever possible. In addition, written documents such as newspaper and magazine articles, annual reports, memoranda, and budgets and other internal information sources were used to provide background information and to corroborate facts mentioned in the interviews.

FIGURE 5
Sample Design—Companies

MANAGEMENT COMPLEXITY

		Low	High
	No	Design Associates	Metal Manufacturing Company
Crisis			
	Yes	Home Mortgages	Control Systems, Inc.

Source: Composed by the author.

Initially, the questions were aimed at learning about the interviewee's job and background, the firm's history and management prior to the professional president's appointment, the impact of the appointment on the relationships in the firm, and the firm's management methods. As the field work progressed, the questions became directed to, and tied into, the evolving description and explanations of the transition.

At all the firms, the owner-founder, the president, board members, and top executives (those one or two levels below the president) were interviewed. An effort was made to interview a wide sample of the executive group—senior as well as new employees, older as well as younger, those who supported the president and those who resisted him. Many executives were interviewed several times. This proved necessary in companies where there was conflict between the owner-founder and the president.

Notes were taken during all interviews and checked soon afterward for their completeness. An effort was made to record the exact words used by the managers. In order to assure reliability of the interview data, all factual statements were cross-checked with documents or, when possible, with data from other interviews. As a rule, the same questions were asked of all who would be in a position to reply to them. Consequently, it was possible to cross-check most of a given interview with several other interviews. Furthermore, upon completion of the writing, a copy of the text was given to an individual appointed by each company to ascertain that this work correctly depicted the management succession at that company.

Initial entry into the four companies was made possible by a sponsor who considered the topic of this study to be sufficiently important to warrant the firm's investment of many management hours. In each firm, the sponsor was a powerful person. At Home Mortgages, the sponsors were the owner-founder and a board member. At Control Systems, Inc., the sponsor was the president. At Design Associates, one of the two owner-founders, Bruce Wallace, was the sponsor. At Metal Manufacturing Company, it was Thomas Gregg, the chairman of the board.

During the second stage of research, some further investigation of literature was done in coordination with the field work. This was triggered by the patterns of response or the anomalies found in the data.

DEFINITION OF TERMS

Early in the field work at the four sites, it became evident that outside presidents had a professional style of management. This phenomenon was corroborated by expert interviews and examination of cases. Since the difference in the management styles of the owner-founder and the presidents was identified as a major source of friction between the two men, the term "outside president" was replaced by "professional president." In the context of this work, this term applies to a president who is not a relative of the owner-founder and who has a professional style of management. The professional president can be either one of the firm's employees who is promoted to president or an outsider who is hired for this position. Throughout the present study, unless specified otherwise, the term "president" refers to the new president who has replaced the owner-founder, and not to the owner-founder.

"Executives" denotes those employees one or two levels below the president on the organization chart. The term "managers" is all-inclusive, as it refers to the owner-founder, the president, and the executives.

OVERVIEW OF THE CHAPTERS

This study is organized so as to depict the succession process in a chronological manner. Traditionally, studies that use exploratory methodology devote entire chapters to the presentation of the data regarding each site and follow with a few chapters presenting the findings. This study emphasizes findings rather than the presentation of data.

The chapters are organized chronologically. Chapter 2 defines entrepreneurial and professional management and discusses a major reason for appointment of a professional president. Chapter 3 discusses the appointment of the professional president: what is the process leading to his appointment and what are the reasons for his appointment? what are the initial reactions and relationships after the president enters the firm? Chapter 4 picks up about three months after the president's appointment and discusses the relationships formed between this time and that of the final outcome. Chapter 5 discusses the final outcome of the transition and presents a framework that explains the differences in developments. Chapter 6 makes recommendations to managers on the basis of the findings and points out future areas of research.

NOTES

1. Simon A. Hershon, "The Problems of Management Succession in Family Businesses" (D.B.A. dissertation, Harvard University, Graduate School of Business Administration, 1976).

2. Abraham Zaleznik and Manfred F. R. Kets de Vries, *Power and the Corporate Mind* (Boston: Houghton Mifflin, 1975), chap. 10; Anne Jardim, *The First Henry Ford: A Study in Personality and Business Leadership (Cambridge: MIT Press, 1970).*

3. Lawrence L. Steinmetz, John B. Kline, and Donald P. Stegall, *Managing the Small Business* (Homewood, Ill.: Richard D. Irwin, 1968), p. 6.

4. Alfred D. Chandler, *Strategy and Structure* (Cambridge: MIT Press, 1962), p. 381.

5. Entrepreneurial and professional styles of management are discussed in Chapter 2.

6. C. Roland Christensen, *Management Succession in Small and Growing Enterprises* (Boston: Division of Research, Harvard University, Graduate School of Business Administration, 1953).

7. Chandler, *Strategy and Structure*, pp. 16–17.

8. Bruce R. Scott, "The Stages of Corporate Development. Part I." (Boston: Intercollegiate Case Clearing House, #9-371-294, (c) 1971).

9. Gordon L. Lippit and Warren H. Schmidt, "Crises in a Developing Organization," *Harvard Business Review* (November–December 1967): 102–12.

10. Larry E. Greiner, "Evolution and Revolution as Organizations Grow," *Harvard Business Review* (July–August 1972): 37–46.

11. Lawrence L. Steinmetz, "Critical Stages of Small Business Growth," *Business Horizons*, February 12, 1969, pp. 29–36.

2

ENTREPRENEURIAL AND PROFESSIONAL MANAGEMENT

Before presenting the definitions of the two management styles named in the title of this chapter, three caveats should be noted. First, the definitions of entrepreneurial and professional management, though closely based on field data, are abstractions of reality. The definitions identify extremes, whereas the management style of most managers falls somewhere between the extremes. Nonetheless, most managers have a sufficient number of one style's characteristics for them to be readily identified as either entrepreneurial or professional managers. Secondly, it should be emphasized that, although most owner-founders have an entrepreneurial style of management, some owner-founders, such as Thomas Gregg of Metal Manufacturing Company, have a professional management style. The term entrepreneurial or professional "manager" is used in these definitions to prevent the identification of any one management style with that of the owner-founder. Finally, although the definitions of entrepreneurial and professional management styles are primarily based on an analysis of the behavior patterns of the company's owner-founders or presidents, these definitions may be applicable in discussing the style of managers at lower levels of the firm and the nature of their relations to their subordinates.

ENTREPRENEURIAL MANAGEMENT

The most distinctive characteristic of the entrepreneurial manager is that he is involved with the operations problems of the firm on a routine basis rather than by exception. The implicit delegation contract between him and his subordinates is that he reserves the right to influence *directly* any decisions that are of importance or interest to him, regardless of the organization level of these decisions. The entrepreneurial manager's subordinates acknowledge his right to make decisions in any area and at any level. At one company, an executive verbalized his understanding of the entrepreneurial owner-founder's view of this contract:

> It's my business, and it's my prerogative to run it as I see fit. My personal future is dependent upon decisions made at all levels of the firm. So, it's my prerogative to go to whatever level I see fit and to make decisions at whatever level I see fit.

This attitude leads the entrepreneurial manager to be greatly involved with detail and the "nitty gritty," as several executives put it. Determining the size of petty cash or directing that all intercompany memos should use "Re" rather than "Subject" are some of the decisions that entrepreneurial presidents of multimillion-dollar organizations make.

The delegation contract discussed above is the core characteristic of the entrepreneurial style of management. It interacts with the planning, structure, evaluation and reward, and control systems used by the entrepreneurial manager to form an internally consistent style of management appropriate for the early stage of development in most firms. The individual characteristics of entrepreneurial management will be discussed below.

The entrepreneurial manager does not rely extensively on plans to provide direction to the executives. Thus, one entrepreneurial manager, Mr. Howard Head, founder of Head Ski, stated:

> I think that this is typical of the kind of business that starts solely from an entrepreneurial product basis, with no interest and skills in management or business in the original package. Such a business never stops to plan. The consuming interest is to build something new and to get acceptance. The entrepreneur has to pick up the rudiments of finance and organizational practices as he goes along. Any thought of planning comes later. Initially, he is solely concerned with the problems of surviving and building. Also, if the business is at all successful, it is so successful that there is no real motivation to stop and obtain the sophisticated planning and people-management techniques.[1]

The entrepreneurial manager's viewpoint regarding financial planning is predominantly short-range and reactive. Authors such as Krentzman, Klein, and Buchele have discussed the short-range viewpoint of the entrepreneurial manager and its threat to the enterprise's survival.[2] The chief financial officer at one firm described their financial planning under the owner-founder in this way:

> We cover expenses on a thirty-day unit basis. The business is a forced
> success each month. Each month is regarded as an independent segment.
> We worry about sixty days from now forty-two days from now.

When the firm does have explicit plans, they are formulated by the
entrepreneurial manager with only little input from other managers. One
executive described the formulation of plans this way: "The plans were
handed down from a power up high when the owner-founder was president."
In Control Systems Inc., the planning process was described in this manner:
"With Kelly, he'd come up with the plans if there were any.... He did not
respect nor get the inputs of other people."

In firms where formal plans are formulated, they are rarely used to direct
managers. An executive at Control Systems stated: "Plans were put together
because the board expected us to have plans and, once formed, they were
forgotten." In some firms, the plans are not sufficiently detailed to guide or
coordinate executive action. In other cases, plans are changed too rapidly to
provide executives with direction. Referring to the time when the entrepreneurial owner-founder was the president, one executive stated:

> We never knew where we were going. If sales were down one week,
> the next week the plan would be changed. Or else, if the sales were up, the
> next week the plan would be changed also. So, we never knew what
> direction we were really headed for.

The lack of explicit plans or their insufficiency of detail and constant change
make the plans useless for directing executives' actions. Thus, the executives
are compelled to check the major decisions facing them with the entrepreneurial manager to assure their being in accordance with the entrepreneurial manager's implicit objectives.

Under entrepreneurial managers, plans are either not made at all or are
not used. It follows that management reward and evaluation are not based on
performance as measured by plans. Rather, the entrepreneurial manager
evaluates and compensates his subordinates on the basis of implicit criteria
and in an informal manner. One executive described an entrepreneurial
owner-founder's attitude to evaluation in this way: "We never had an
appraisal of performance. We never had reviews.... The problem is that we
never knew how we were reviewed." An executive at another company
described the evaluation process under the entrepreneurial owner-founder in
this way:

> We have no system of rewards and no evaluation system.... Some
> run a business so that you can evaluate the people and say to them, "This

is how you are evaluated." That is not being done here.... We get a raise when we ask for it. There is no periodic evaluation. When you want a raise, you ask for it, and if you've done something to deserve it, you'll get it. [The owner-founder] is fond of saying that this is not a factory where you have periodic evaluations and raises. You have to do something to deserve a raise.

Family relations and loyalty to employees with seniority often figure significantly in the entrepreneurial manager's decisions on employment or promotion of personnel. In some instances, family relations may be as important a factor as competence in an owner-founder's promotion of an employee. In such instances, owner-founders often equate their personal interest with the firm's interest. Or, if they are aware of the divergence between their personal desires and what is in the firm's interest, they give priority to their personal desires. Some executives accept such priority as legitimate. The reaction of other executives to such promotions is illustrated by the following composite:

> Such promotions would never be made on the open market. The most important qualification in these situations is being a relative of the owner-founder. Furthermore, the owner-founder does not tolerate criticism of such promotions. "Who are you to tell me about my relatives?" He does not listen. It's a family affair, and if you say anything, you will be in trouble. No one can criticize the family.

Seniority also plays a major part in decisions made by entrepreneurial managers. An executive at one firm made the following observation with which the other executives agreed:

> There is a lot of paternalism in this company, and by that, I don't mean nepotism. There is a lot of keeping people around because they have seniority, though they may not be the most competent people.

Rather than relying on formal control systems, the entrepreneurial manager relies predominantly on frequent informal talks and participation in operating decisions to keep informed and to guide executives. The chief financial officer at one site stated: "We are very loose in the control area because this firm is viewed from the owner-founder's viewpoint as a small firm. Corporate policies and guidelines are non-existent." Commenting on his methods of management as chairman of the board, one owner-founder stated: "When I come in in the morning, I call several buyers or merchandisers and spend fifteen minutes talking to each of them." In fact, this person spent the majority of his time "kibbitzing with the boys." The following statements were made in reference to the owner-founders of two companies:

He doesn't set formal meetings to discuss things. We do not wait until a formal meeting to do something. As the thought hits him, he runs down the hall and discusses it immediately, If he sees me and we discuss something that involves Jack, then he will run to see Jack after me. He doesn't wait until Wednesday at 2 o'clock. The president had meetings.

He should create a committee and have people report to him on a regular formalized basis. Now he runs back and forth and asks people what is going on.

Although all managers rely on oral communication, the entrepreneurial manager tends to use it in a less planned and formal manner than does the professional manager.

Rather than establishing formal control systems to obtain information about the internal operations of the firm, the entrepreneurial manager tends to rely on informal sources. For example, several of the entrepreneurial owner-founders that were studied relied on personally opening all the mail received by the company each day to "keep on top of what's happening." Another counted the orders that came in each day to determine the firm's financial position.

In all firms managed by an entrepreneurial manager the de facto structure of the firm can be best characterized as a pinwheel, with the entrepreneurial manager in the center and executives as much as four levels below him forming the spikes (Figure 6, part A). If there are any written organization charts, they are not adhered to by the entrepreneurial manager. He often gives direct instructions to individuals at any level in the organization. Although each subordinate manager may structure his area in a regular hierarchical manner, he knows that the entrepreneurial manager reserves the right to go around him and to make decisions at any level (Figure 6, part B).

Studies by Greiner, Hershon, and George Strauss also discuss the individual characteristics of the entrepreneurial management style.[3] The definition presented here, however, emphasizes entrepreneurial management as a group of interrelated characteristics forming an internally consistent style of management. The core characteristic of entrepreneurial management is the entrepreneurial president's involvement in operating decisions on a routine basis. The firm's wheel-shaped organization structure and frequent informal interactions between the entrepreneurial manager and his subordinates result from this core characteristic. Similarly, when the manager is routinely involved in operating decisions, he does not need to rely on plans to direct managers and evaluate them, or on formal control systems, in order to be informed of the company's operations (Figure 7). Furthermore, the secondary characteristics of entrepreneurial management are consistent with each other and reinforce each other. For example, the paucity of formal

FIGURE 6

Organization Structure with Entrepreneurial Management

E = Executives

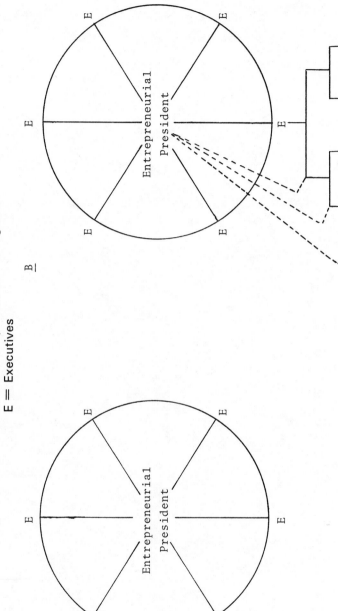

Source: Constructed by the author.

19

FIGURE 7
Entrepreneurial Management

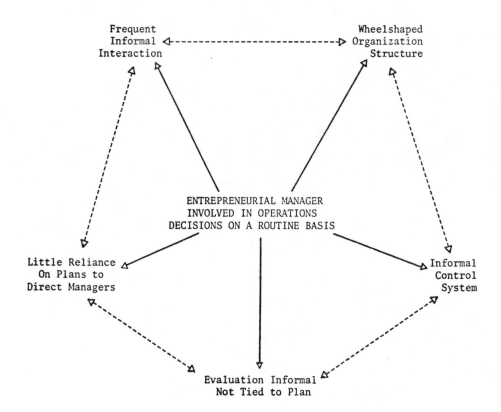

Source: Constructed by the author.

measurement systems or plans for directing managers leads to an informal and intuitive evaluation system.

PROFESSIONAL MANAGEMENT

As in the case of entrepreneurial management, the predominant attribute of professional management is the delegation contract between the professional manager and his subordinates. The subordinates have the right to make decisions in their own areas as long as they act and perform in accordance with a plan. The following statement was typical of those made by executives working for a professional president:

Q. What is your relationship to Mr. Madanick?
A. I answer directly to Steve. Everybody has a different management style. Steve's overall philosophy is to put people in charge of areas and leave it up to them to run their area in accordance with the basic overall plan. If there is a problem, he'll get involved in discussions. Otherwise, you're left to run your own part of the business in your own way. Steve gets involved in the overall policy and overall management goals. The exact details are left to the department heads.

The professional manager intervenes in decisions, falling within a subordinate's area of responsibility only when there is a variance between performance and the written goals or when the subordinate himself requests it. Ryan, the professional president at Metal Manufacturing, stated:

The manufacturing process is a simple one, but it gets out of control so fast that it will make your head spin.... I personally spent January and February setting up guidelines for each plant.... It was doing well for ten months, and then, I thought well, this guy [VP of Operations] knows what he's doing. I told him that I won't dash back to help him and I'm going to withdraw from involvement in his area.

When asked to compare his style with the style of Home Mortgages' professional president, Joseph Samuels stated:

We're two different kinds of operators. I grew up in this business. I came up from operations to become the chairman of the Board. I am totally involed in the smallest piece of merchandising, the smallest piece of advertising. I am always questioning. Mr. Madanick, however, depends on the men who run the business to run it, and they're expected to come to him if they have a problem.

The professional managers use writtten plans, formal evaluation and reward systems, and formal structure in order to enable the managers to make decisions and in order to direct their decisions.

Plans are seen as a crucial tool by the professional manager for guiding the actions of executives. Executives participate in determining the company's plans. Thus, the executives know the plan and, having participated in its formulation, are committed to it. In addition, the plan is sufficiently detailed to be useful to the executives.

> We have been setting up budgets. Now we know in black and white in advance what our budget is going to be, and it is broken down for different products. We know where we are headed.... I get a weekly report comparing my planned budget with actual expenses. And I compare the two to determine if we are going over the budget.

Finally, as compared to the situation under an entrepreneurial manager, the plan is changed less often in order that executives may use it.

The professional manager employs evaluation and rewards to motivate his subordinate to accomplish the organization's objective. In comparison to entrepreneurial managers, the criteria used for evaluation are more explicit and better communicated to subordinates. In Metal Manufacturing and Home Mortgages, the professional presidents closely tied in evaluation and rewards with fulfillment of objectives.

> We had long-range plans before, but planning is more disciplined now. The disciplined part is that we are evaluated very carefully on how we do relative to the plan. We're supposed to accomplish those things in the plan, and the basis for our annual appraisal and bonus is how we do relative to the plan.

The professional manager relies on written control systems to a much greater extent than the entrepreneurial manager does. Whereas the entrepreneurial manager relies predominantly on oral communication to provide him with the basic data relating to the firm's performance, the professional manager relies more on written reports. Joseph Samuels, the entrepreneurial owner-founder of Home Mortgages, stated:

> I have an open door policy. That doesn't only mean that they [the executives] can come see me when they want to. When I come in the morning, I call them and ask them to come up and talk with me. I go down and sit and talk with the merchandisers or buyers and have coffee and talk. When Mr. Madanick comes in in the morning, he sits at his desk and opens his mail and reads it.

In contrast to the entrepreneurial manager, the professional manager relies more on facts and figures than on intuition. Furthermore, since he is not involed in day-to-day operating decisions, he needs an alternative source of information. Consequently, the professional manager needs and uses formal reports, financial and nonfinancial, to keep informed.

The professional manager establishes an organization structure more formal than the kind favored by the entrepreneurial manager. Furthermore, the professional manager observes the line of authority more fully than does the entrepreneurial manager. He seldom goes around his subordinates to make suggestions to lower level managers about operating details. The professional manager uses formal meetings and committees to integrate different areas of the firm to a greater extent than is done by the entrepreneurial manager. Thus, both he and the executives can know what is occurring in all of the areas of operations.

An entrepreneurial manager's approach to managing is very different from that of a professional manager. Whereas the former manages by "doing," by personally making operations decisions, the latter manages primarily by enabling other managers to act. Comparing Peter Davis, the professional president of Control Systems, with John Kelly, its entrepreneurial owner-founder, one executive stated: "Pete doesn't make decisions. He is more of a manager than a creator or a motivator. John is more of a doer. Pete doesn't do. He manages people that do. John did."

It should be emphasized that professional management is an internally consistent method of managing a firm. The core characteristic of professional management is the professional manager's involvement in operations decisions by exception (that is to say, when there is a deviation from plan) rather than on a routine basis. Formal plans are required to direct the subordinates, and formal control systems are required to keep the professional manager informed of his subordinates' activities. Since the professional manager relies on his subordinates to implement plans, he must motivate them to act in accordance with the plans. Consequently, they are allowed to participate in the formulation of plans and are evaluated on the basis of their performance relative to the plan. Finally, the professional manager refrains from becoming involved in operations decisions, something which leads to a more formal organizational structure (Figure 8). As is the case with the definition of entrepreneurial management, the secondary characteristics of professional management are self-reinforcing. For example, one cannot evaluate managers based on performance against plans unless such formal plans are established and unless information regarding the individual's performance is provided by a measurement system. A similar relationship exists among the other characteristics of professional management.

MANAGEMENT STYLE AND THE FIRM'S DEVELOPMENT

The entrepreneurial style of management is effective in the early stages of the firm's growth. The small number and physical proximity of employees

FIGURE 8
Professional Management

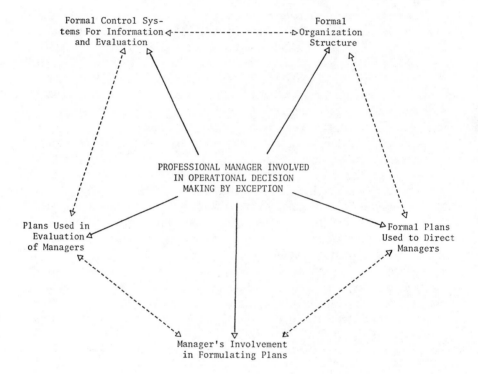

Source: Constructed by the author.

permit the entrepreneurial owner-founder to rely primarily on face-to-face oral communications. The firm's operations are small enough so that the entrepreneurial owner-founder has enough time to have an input into, if not control of, all operating decisions.

Typically, in the early phase of an organization's existence, the owner-founder personally manages one or more areas of the firm. The company's product or service is usually based on the owner-founder's competence and is therefore easily understood by him. The organization structure is informal. Talking about the first Henry Ford's style of management, Jardim states:

> There was still so much to be done that the issue of overlapping jurisdictions was less a problem than a source for strength. Hawkins [Norval Hawkins, in charge of sales], for example, introduced the first comprehensive accounting system, and Lee [John R. Lee, responsible for personnel] carried it further. Wills's [C. H. Wills, whose main function was design engineering] contributions ranged from work on the design of the cars to metallurgy to the design of machine tools. He was concerned with purchasing, with make-or-buy decisions and with pricing policy.[4]

The organization is an informal group with the owner-founder playing a central role in the company.

The tragedy of the entrepreneurial owner-founder lies in the fact that, as the organization grows in size and complexity, the very style of management which brought about the firm's growth and success becomes an impediment to its continued success and development. In *The New Industrial State*, John Kenneth Galbraith remarks: "The great entrepreneur must, in fact, be compared in life with the male *Apis Mellifera*. He accomplishes his act of conception at the price of his own extinction."[5]

As the organization grows, the number of decisions exceeds the time available to the entrepreneurial owner-founder for dealing with them. Furthermore, the number of employees becomes so large that the entrepreneurial owner-founder does not have the time to talk with them frequently enough to give them direction. Due to the increasing number and diversity of products, the entrepreneurial owner-founder faces increasingly complicated questions that require more careful deliberation on his part. Dealing with these complexities may in some cases be beyond his skills or competence. The firm's growth thus renders entrepreneurial mmanagement inappropriate and obsolete.

Numerous authors concur that as a company grows in size and complexity, the nature of the problems facing it and the type of management required by it change. Lippit and Schmidt as well as Greiner view organization development as a series of crises, the earlier ones centering on survival of the firm and the later ones centering on management's ability to adapt to the growth requirements of the firm.[6] Chandler, Scott, Clifford, Steinmetz, and Salter each identify the stages of the firm's growth.[7] They concur that growth brings about increasing decentralization of decision making and increasingly rational and formal organization patterns, such as formalized structure and reporting relations, written policies and objectives, and evaluation criteria. Chandler's conclusion in *Strategy and Structure* represents the viewpoints of the second group of authors:

> Volume expansion, geographical dispersion, vertical integration, product diversification, and continued growth by any of these basic strategies laid an increasingly heavy load of entrepreneurial decision making on the senior executive. If they failed to re-form the lines of authority and communication to develop information necessary for administration, the executives throughout the organization were drawn deeper and deeper into operational activities and often were working at cross purposes to and in conflict with one another.[8]

The Decision to Grow in Complexity

The results of this study agree with the above authors that increasing growth in size and complexity mandates a change in the style by which the firm is managed. It should be pointed out, though, that such a mandatory change may be avoided by choosing *not* to grow in size and complexity. In making this decision, the entrepreneurial owner-founder may be faced with two sets of considerations.

Factors external to the owner-founder influence his decision regarding the company's growth in size and complexity. First, the firm's technology may necessitate large volume for the firm to benefit from economies of scale and remain competitive. Secondly, market demands may require a larger product line. Finally, the expectations and demands of the investors and employees of the enterprise must be considered. What are the stockholders' expectations for the company's growth? What would be the repercussions of the decision on the firm's ability to attract and retain high caliber employees?

The personal considerations of the owner-founder may also influence his decisions regarding the company's growth. All owner-founders studied supported growth in size and the expansion of the firm into new areas of business. Work done by Collins and Moore, Kets de Vries, and McClelland corroborates this finding.

One of the owner-founder's personal reasons for pursuing a strategy of growth is monetary benefit. Increased sales and net worth denote personal monetary gain for the owner(s) of the firm. Financial motivation, though, is often only a partial explanation of the owner-founder's pursuit of growth. The marginal benefit of increased income becomes very low after a certain point. Most of the owner-founders studied were very wealthy. One executive described the owner-founder of his firm thus: "He could retire tomorrow and would not even go through a fraction of [his] wealth if [he] didn't earn another penny."

If monetary gain is not the primary motivation for the owner-founder's preference for growth, then what is? One executive described Bruce Wallace's motivation in this way:

> In psychology, there is a thing called "free floating anxiety." That's as opposed to specific anxieties where you are anxious about a specific thing like a meeting or a family problem. But sometimes, you get up in the morning, and you just feel anxious, and your stomach feels rotten, and you don't know why. I think that, just like there is free-floating anxiety, there is non-specific free-floating hunger—whatever comes to you is not enough. You always have a desire for more. You weren't necessarily saying you were going to achieve something, but you just have this insatiable desire. This is Bruce's characteristic.

This same characteristic is discussed at length by David C. McClelland in *The Achieving Society*.[9] McClelland's main finding on this subject, as recorded in a shorter study, is that a high need for achievement is an essential characteristic for entrepreneurial success.[10] Because of their close identification with the firm, the owner-founders view the firm's growth as a measure of personal achievement. Perhaps due to this identification, they pursue a policy of more sales, more employees, and more offices or branches.

Kets de Vries and Collins and Moore bear out the above explanation for the owner-founders' desire for growth. On the basis of a psychoanalytic study, Kets de Vries concludes that "a feeling of dissatisfaction remains as a continuous harassment for the entrepreneur."[11] Collins and Moore, in a psychological study of entrepreneurs, state:

> The result is that the entrepreneur is left with a feeling of never being quite able to reach any satisfactory definable and rewarding goal. His response to this is a renewed striving for further, equally unsatisfactory goals. Hence, his feeling of restlessness and need to move on to new fields. In the eyes of his associates, however, he is apt to be perceived as a man who never rests content with past successes, but who must ever strive anew for additional triumphs.[12]

The Owner-Founders' Inability to Change Their Style of Management

The entrepreneurial owner-founder who, whether for personal or other reasons, decides to pursue a strategy of growth must change his management style at some point during the firm's development.

The large majority of the entrepreneurial owner-founders do *not* make the transition to a professional style of management. The venture capitalists interviewed stated that an entrepreneurial owner-founder seldom adapts his management style to the changing needs of the firm. Among the present study's entrepreneurial owner-founders, none had been able to make the transition to a professional style of management. In *Strategy and Structure*, Chandler states:

> This short survey not only stresses that expansion did cause administrative problems which led, in time, to organization change and readjustment, but it further suggests that the essential reshaping of administrative structure nearly always had to wait for a change in the top command. Clearly many empire builders—those industrialists who initially brought vast numbers of men, and amounts of money and of materials, under a single corporate roof—had relatively little interest in devising schemes to assure a more efficient overall management of these resources. Henry Ford, Walter P. Chrysler, Orlando J. Weber, Herbert H. and Willard H. Dow, Harry J. Sinclair, Captain Alfred E. Hunt and his son, Roy A. Hunt of Alcoa, Stephen T. Birch of Kennecott, Cornelius F. Kelley of Anaconda, Elbert H. Gray of United States Steel, Ernest J. Wier of National Steel, Camille Dreyfus of Celanese, and Paul W. Litchfield of Goodyear, all had much the same lack of concern about systematic administration as had William C. Durant, Richard Sears, and Coleman du Pont.[13]

Chandler's "structure," which he defines as lines of authority and communication and the information that flows through these lines, is a large component of management style.

The owner-founder does not change his style of management for various reasons. When the firm was started, the owner-founder had to perform most of the firm's functions himself and had to be involved in operations in order for the firm to survive. He often took care of several functional areas. He was the salesman or the designer or the accountant. He did not have the staff to delegate to. Consequently, he developed a habit of being involved with what, to a professional manager, is "detail." Such habits are hard to break. Furthermore, the entrepreneurial owner-founder has the skills to manage in an entrepreneurial manner but may not have the skills or knowledge to establish and use formal control systems and reports. Usually, the origins of the businesses rest on excellence in one functional specialty rather than in administrative ability. Recalling the founding of Head Ski Company, Mr. Howard Head remarked:

> When I started out, I was a mechanical design engineer—the whole origin of the business was that it should be possible to build a better ski. What started as an engineering puzzle ended as a business.[14]

Even if he has the opportunity and capability of acquiring new skills required for professional management, the owner-founder may resist this step because he wishes to maintain his involvement with the operations and the day-to-day activity of the organization. There are three reasons for this. First, the owner-founder may believe that his withdrawal from the operations could hurt the firm. This reason may be valid in those firms where the client relationships and the product are heavily dependent on the owner-founder. Secondly, the owner-founder may maintain his involvement in operations decision making because he views withdrawing from operations decisions to signify that the firm can dispense with his contributions.

Finally, the owner-founder may not want to withdraw from daily operations because he does not trust his subordinates. The executives at two of the sites identified this factor as influencing the owner-founders' behavior. At Control Systems, Inc., many managers made remarks to concur with the following observation, voiced by an executive, about the entrepreneurial owner-founder: "He had a hard time trusting others to run the firm.... His basic makeup was such that he did not trust people." In Design Associates, an executive stated:

> But it is categorically true that Bruce is extremely involved. He is very much involved in every account and in all the major decisions of every account. He doesn't trust others. That's a terrible thing to say, but he doesn't.

Unfortunately, the entrepreneurial style of the owner-founder may reinforce his lack of trust in the executives (Figure 9). Since the owner-founder does not trust his subordinates, he usually either makes the major operations decisions facing the company or has a large input in them. The consequence of this is to discourage independent decision making on the part of the executives. Commenting on the situation at Control Systems while John Kelly was president, Peter Davis said:

> The managers here were afraid to stick their necks out. They would and did, but after a while, they said "To hell with this." For example, the guy in charge of advertising said, "Why should I bother to make new advertising programs when it will all be changed by John in two months anyway?" The treasurer felt the same way. There were a lot of programs that he felt should be implemented, but he knew that John wouldn't do it anyway. So, why bother?

To the entrepreneurial owner-founder, the executives' lack of initiative and independent decision making, in turn, becomes justification for his lack of trust.

FIGURE 9
Dynamics of Entrepreneurial Owner-Founders' Lack of Trust

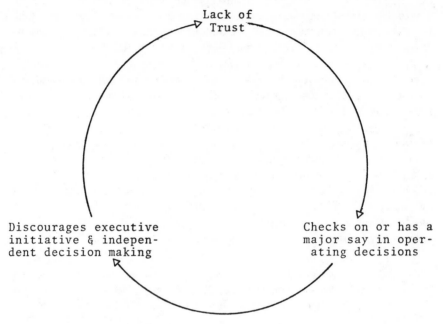

Source: Constructed by the author.

Impact on Firms of Owner-Founders'
Inability to Change

The results of the entrepreneurial owner-founder's inability to adapt his style of management may range from disorder to crisis. As the number of decisions facing the firm increases, the amount of time available to the owner-founder, proportionately restricted, becomes a severe bottleneck for the company. Due to his time, he cannot exert control through direct participation in all the revlevant decisions. Consequently, some areas of the firm are left without direction. Furthermore, since the entrepreneurial owner-founder is the main coordinating mechanism, the pressure on him leads to decreased coordination between areas. Some symptoms of these problems are: increasing frantic activity on the part of the entrepreneurial owner-founder as well as his executives; and financial problems such as increasing cost, decreasing revenue, or poor asset management.

Whether disorder turns to crisis depends on the organization's rate of growth, the degree of the owner-founder's adaptability, as well as a third factor, the firm's economic environment. This last term refers to industry trends as well as general economic conditions. If unfavorable, the economic environment may accelerate crisis. On the other hand, if the economic environment is favorable, it can balance the inefficiencies in the firm's management for some time. Crisis, however, is inevitable once the economic conditions become less favorable. Employing a president is an action often taken by the board and/or the owner-founder as a remedy for disorder or crisis.

NOTES

1. Howard H. Stevenson, "Head Ski Company, Inc." (Boston, Massachusetts: Intercollegiate Case Clearing House, #6-313-120, (c) 1967), p. 21.

2. Harvey C. Krentzman, *Managing for Profits* (Washington, D.C.: Government Printing Office, 1968); Howard J. Klein, *Stop! You're Killing the Business* (New York: Mason & Lipscomb, 1975); Robert B. Buchele, *Business Policy in Growing Firms* (San Francisco: Chandler, 1967).

3. Larry E. Greiner, "Evolution and Revolution as Organizations Grow," *Harvard Business Review* (July–August 1972): 37–46; Simon A. Hershon, "The Problems of Management Succession in Family Businesses (D.B.A. dissertation, Harvard University, Graduate School of Business Administration, 1976); George Strauss, "Adolescence in Organizational Growth: Problems, Pains, Possibilities," *Organizational Dynamics* (Spring 1974): 3–17.

4. Anne Jardim, *The First Henry Ford: A Study in Personality and Business Leadership* (Cambridge: MIT Press, 1970), p. 85.

5. John Kenneth Galbraith, *The New Industrial State* (Boston: Houghton Mifflin, 1971), p. 89.

6. Gordon L. Lippit and Warren H. Schmidt, "Crises in a Developing Organization," *Harvard Business Review* (November–December 1967): 110–12; Greiner, "Evolution and Revolution", pp. 37–46.

7. Donald K. Clifford, Jr., "Growth Pains of the Threshold Company," *Harvard Business Review* (September–October 1973): 143–54; Lawrence L. Steinmetz, "Critical Stages of Small Business Growth," *Business Horizons*, February 12, 1969, pp. 29–36; Malcolm L. Salter, "Stages of Corporate Development: Implications for Management Control" (D.B.A. dissertation, Harvard University, Graduate School of Business Administration, 1968).

8. Alfred D. Chandler, *Strategy and Structure* (Cambridge: MIT Press, 1962), p. 315.

9. David C. McClelland, *The Achieving Society* (New York: Free Press, 1961).

10. David C. McClelland, "Achievement Motivation Can Be Developed," *Harvard Business Review* (November–December 1965): 6–24. McClelland defines the need for achievement in this manner: "The need for achievement is measured by coding a person's spontaneous thoughts, as in the imaginative stories he tells, for the frequency with which he thinks about competing with a standard of excellence or doing something better than before."

11. Manfred F. R. Kets de Vries, "Myth and Reality of Entrepreneurship" (Boston: Working Paper #4-471-031, Harvard Business School, (c) 1970).

12. Orvis Collins and David G. Moore, *The Organization Makers* (New York: Appleton-Century-Crofts, 1970).

13. Chandler, *Strategy and Structure*, p. 380.

14. Howard H. Stevenson, "Head Ski Company" p. 8.

3

APPOINTMENT OF THE PROFESSIONAL PRESIDENT

A synopsis of the history of each company aids in understanding the reasons for appointment of the president, the actions leading to the president's appointment, and the initial reactions of the different parties.

HOME MORTGAGES COMPANY

Owner-founder Joseph Samuels started his mortgage banking operations, which have specialized in residential operations, in California in 1947. During the next ten years, he opened six additional loan origination offices. One of his relatives was made a partner in charge of each new office that was established. In 1960, Home Mortgages sold stock to the public in order to obtain funds for additional growth. Between 1961 and 1971, the company went through a period of rapid growth opening a total of 20 new loan origination offices. By 1971, Home Mortgages had over $6,000,000 in revenues. At this time, Samuels and his family owned approximately 18 percent of the firm's equity; the remainder of the stock was widely dispersed.

Samuels had been both president and chairman of the board of directors of Home Mortgages since its founding. In 1971, when he reached the age of 63, he agreed to the board's request that a new president be appointed. A member of Samuels' family, Barry Stein, was chosen as president despite the board's reluctance towards this appointment. Samuels himself continued to serve as chairman and chief executive officer.

By 1974, the company had fallen into severe financial difficulties. Barry

Stein resigned and Samuels resumed the president's post. Samuels spent the better part of the next eight months negotiating with banks and creditors in his resolve to save the firm from bankruptcy. While Home Mortgages was experiencing this financial crisis, Samuels and Home Mortgages' board of directors began interviewing candidates for the presidency of the firm.

CONTROL SYSTEMS INC.

In contrast to Home Mortgages, Control Systems is a young enterprise, founded in 1967 by John Kelly. The firm designs and produces measuring instruments used in process control systems. Kelly ran out of cash before the design problems of the company's first product were solved. Consequently, he had to sell 65 percent of the company's equity to National Capital Corporation (NCC), a holding company. NCC appointed Kelly as president and member of the board of directors. He was given a two-year employment contract with compensation in the form of salary and stock options tied into the profitability of Control Systems.

In 1972, due to the need for additional financing, NCC sold some of the stock it then held to two venture capital firms. This transaction resulted in the following ownership profile: NCC, 40 percent, John Kelly, 25 percent, and the two venture capital firms, 35 percent. The stockholders all served on the board of directors. Two seats were held by NCC's owners, two by representatives of the two venture capital firms, and one seat by Kelly himself. By 1974, Control Systems' sales had reached $3.8 million, having averaged a growth of 74 percent per year.

In spite of Control Systems' satisfactory financial performance, severe disagreements developed between Kelly and the other board members. These disagreements centered around several issues. First of all, in the board's view, Kelly did not adequately consult with them prior to making significant commitments on the firm's behalf. For example, the board members believed that Kelly committed NCC to acquire another company prior to complete disclosure of his intentions to the board. In another instance, Kelly obligated the company to a major investment in facilities without early consultation with the board; the board found itself in the position of having no alternative but to approve Kelly's actions. Secondly, the board was dissatisfied with Kelly's style of management. In their opinion, he did not develop the abilities of the firm's executives and did not himself have the attributes necessary to manage the firm's future growth. Thirdly, the board believed that Kelly was making decisions that were for his personal gain and not to the long-term advantage of the company.

Kelly, on the other hand, felt that the board involved itself too closely in the company's operations. Furthermore, he believed that the board's primary objective was to benefit NCC, the holding company that owned 40 percent of the company, rather than to benefit Control Systems. One executive described the relationshp thus: "John didn't trust them. So, he didn't give them information. Because of that, they didn't trust him. It was like a spiral."

In 1974, the board members approached Kelly about hiring an executive vice president. Kelly was reluctant to agree to this course of action, but he relented upon the board's decision that his own salary would be maintained in spite of this new expense. The board hired Peter Davis, who had previously served as president of another company owned by NCC. Three months later, the board promoted Davis to president of Control Systems, and Kelly became the chairman of the board.

DESIGN ASSOCIATES

Design Associates is an industrial design firm that specializes in developing corporate identity for companies such as airlines, through designing logos, stationery, annual reports, employee uniforms and interior office design. Design Associates was founded in 1968 when Bruce Wallace and Carl Slattery set up a phone and a desk on the porch of Wallace's home and began soliciting clients. By 1975, Design Associates was located in elegant offices in Manhattan, and it employed 76 employees. Between 1968 and 1975, the firm's sales growth averaged over 50 percent per year, and reached $25 million in revenues by 1975. The founders' philosophy was: "It's better to have a small share of a big pie than half a tart." Presently, Wallace and Slattery each own 29 percent of the firm's equity, the remainder being dispersed among 30 of the firm's executives.

Prior to hiring a new president, Slattery was primarily responsible for the design function of the firm, and Wallace, for sales and client relationships. The executives interviewed considered Wallace the dominant member of the pair.

Wallace has a predominantly entrepreneurial style of management. As the firm grew, however, not even 12- to 16-hour workdays were sufficient to perform all the work Wallace believed needed his personal involvement. Consequently, some problems and some clients received brief and inadequate attention.

In order to alleviate these problems and bring management depth to the company, Bill Cooper was hired in March 1976 as president of the company. Wallace became chief executive officer and chairman of the board, and Slattery retained his position as director of design and also vice-chairman.

METAL MANUFACTURING COMPANY

Metal Manufacturing Company manufactures metallic parts to customer specifications through the use of a complex manufacturing process.

The firm was founded in 1951 and had grown to $150 million in sales by 1975. Thomas Gregg managed the firm in close collaboration with his father until 1966, when his father passed away. The elder Gregg had served as chairman of the board, while his son served as president. A longtime director at Metal Manufacturing described their working relationship in this way.

> Mr. Gregg, Senior, attended all of the meetings of the Board. Tom listened to every word he said, and he got good advice. Mr. Gregg had very little involvement in operating type decisions. He involved himself in things such as foreign licensing, financing, and questions like "Should we build a new plant?"

Thomas Gregg has a professional style of management. "Hire competent people, and let them do the job" was the philosophy underlying his management, according to several board members and executives.

In the early 1960s, the demand for Metal Manufacturing's products outgrew its manufacturing capacity. Consequently, in 1965, new plants were built by obtaining financing from a group of venture capitalists. This financing resulted in the dilution of the family's ownership to 50 percent, with the venture capitalists owning 25 percent of the equity and the remainder of the stock being held by board members, employees, and a few outsiders. A new vice-president of manufacturing was hired in 1967 to solve the increasing problems in the firm's manufacturing process. The plan was for the new vice-president to gradually assume additional responsibility for other functions and eventually to become the executive vice-president of Metal Manufacturing. After one year, however, it was obvious to the company's executives that he lacked the decision-making ability necessary to accomplish his task, and subsequently he left the firm.

In 1970, David Ryan was hired as executive vice-president with the understanding on the part of Gregg and the board of directors that he would be promoted to president after five years of satisfactory service.

ROLE OF THE OWNER-FOUNDER
IN THE APPOINTMENT PROCESS

Succession poses difficult personal problems for most owner-founders. Their reaction to giving up the president's post is influenced by emotional and financial considerations. Whether and how they reconcile these factors determines their role in appointing a new president. The emotional considerations that may influence owner-founders' view of succession are: their perception of their importance to the company and their concern about being replaced; the importance of the firm to their self-concept; the impact of the new appointment on their activities; and their ability to deal with the idea of death. Each of these points will be discussed below, and then will follow a description of the financial considerations influencing the owner-founders' role in the appointment process.

Owner-founders often perceive themselves as the key individuals in the organization. It is because of owner-founders' creativity, hard work, sacrifice, and willingness to take risks that their firms became reality. Owner-founders consider themselves important not only to the creation of the companies but to their continued survival and success. "They [the board members] feel the image of this firm would be hurt if the president resigned. There is no way that this firm can be hurt, unless I resign," stated an owner-founder at one site. In the case of competent owner-founders, this attitude is often reinforced by the firm's employees or outsiders. In an article about Arlen Realty Company and its owner-founder, Arthur Cohen, Eleanor Carruth writes: "to many Arlen is Cohen. 'If Arthur were in an airplane crash,' remarks one real estate executive, 'I'd sell before the plane touched ground.' "[1]

Some owner-founders' doubts about other people's ability to replace them, therefore, follow at least partly from their perception of their importance to the company. If, as the owner-founder believes, his function and expertise are so crucial to the organization, then, how can another person perform this function as well as he? He has worked in the organization longer than anyone else. His initial responsibilities encompassed all of the firm's activities, from answering all phone calls to raising capital. He knows the company's history, policies, and business better than anyone else. Consequently, he is often annoyed at others' assumptions that they can perform as well as he, let alone replace him. "I am one of the founders of this industry. I've been in this industry for thirty years. No one here can tell me I shouldn't hire a purchasing manager," yelled an owner-founder at executives whose views were at some odds with his. The owner-founder's resistance to the appointment of a professional president increases with the strength of his perception of his own importance to the firm. He sees the president's appointment as diminishing his role in his company and as being proof that he is in fact replaceable.

According to McClelland's *The Achieving Society*, owner-founders are very achievement oriented.[2] To the owner-founder, the company is "a medium for his personal gratification and achievement."[3] A successful company serves as proof of his success and achievement. Wallace's account of Design Associates' history reflects the satisfaction derived from such success:

> In July 1968, I formed Design Associates with Carl Slattery and a secretary and no accounts. Today we are one of the largest industrial design firms in the nation, employ one hundred and five people in five offices, with revenues in excess of $25 million annually.

The firm plays an important role in the self-concept of many owner-founders. It gives some owner-founders the opportunity to view themselves as "industry founders." Samuels frequently used this phrase in his conversations. By using their position in the organization or the income derived from it, owner-founders can obtain public recognition as community leaders or philanthropists. Samuels had plaques that acknowledged his generosity and community involvement covering one wall of his office. In John Kelly's case, his own identification with Control Systems had extended to his family's identification of him. One Father's Day, his children made him a card bearing the inscription: "To the Father of Control Systems Inc."

The owner-founder's attitude toward succession is influenced by his feelings of identification with the firm. To some owner-founders, the appointment of a professional president means that in the future, they will have to share credit for the achievements of the enterprise with another person. Furthermore, they view succession as depriving them of their identity as *the* top manager of their firm. This results in severe distress for these owner-founders. An incident at Home Mortgages illustrates the owner-founder's sensitivity to these issues. After Steve Madanick was hired as president of Home Mortgages, an article appeared in Samuels' home newspaper. Above the article was a large picture of Madanick; little mention of Samuels was made. "That tore him apart," a board member said. Madanick recalled Samuels' reaction: "Mr. Samuels came in and told me, 'We can't work together any more!' I said, 'What happened?' What had happened was that the newspaper had an article in it with my picture." Samuels saw the president usurping his identity as the top man at Home Mortgages. Madanick eventually learned that "the more I can allow him to take the lead in the public eye, the better things are for the company and for myself."

For other owner-founders, their close identification with the company has the opposite effect, that of motivating them to insure a smooth transition to a professional president. The pride and sense of achievement that these owner-founders derive from the company encourages them to be more concerned with preserving the company's good name and success than with retaining their identity as its top manager. According to Levinson,

> For the entrepreneur, the business is essentially an extension of himself, a medium for his personal gratification and achievement above all. And if he is concerned about what happens to his business after he passes on, that concern usually takes the form of thinking of the kind of monument he will leave behind.[4]

The owner-founder of Metal Manufacturing, Thomas Gregg, explained one of his reasons for insuring a smooth transition in this way:

> I don't want to see Metal Manufacturing disappear. Not only from the

financial point of view, but also because of pride. *I* do not want to be faulted if it falls apart. Therefore, I have to provide for management succession.

The third factor influencing owner-founders' attitudes—especially those of more senior owner-founders—toward a new president is the impact the loss of this post will have on their own activities. If an owner-founder has sufficient outside interests or hobbies, he will be able to keep himself occupied should he become chairman of the board or retire after the new president's appointment. Unfortunately, most entrepreneurial owner-founders are forced by their style of management to work increasingly long hours in the interest of their businesses. Thus, they do not have sufficient time to develop or cultivate outside interests. In the case of Thomas Gregg, however, his professional management style had left him with adequate time to develop outside interests. One of his reasons for welcoming a professional president was that this would enable him to spend more time on outside activities. One board member said:

> Tom had other interests. He was interested in our state's affairs, in European relations, and in relations between research and development and manufacturing. That interested him more than dealing with daily operating problems. His interest and genuine commitment are that business owes to society something more than just making money. That suggested a need for somebody to become president.

The final factor influencing the owner-founder's reaction to the appointment of a professional president is a subconscious fear of death, especially if the owner-founder is an older person. In *On Death and Dying*, Kübler-Ross identifies the predominance of the fear of death among humans:

> When we look back in time and study old cultures and people, we are impressed that death has always been distasteful to man and will probably always be. From a psychiatrist's point of view, this is very understandable and can perhaps be best explained by our basic knowledge that, in our unconscious, death is never possible in regard to ourselves.... Death is still a fearful, frightening happening, and the fear of death is a universal fear even if we think we have mastered it on many levels.[5]

Some owner-founders resist appointment of a president because they subconsciously equate giving up the president's job with dying. When asked why he worked ten-hour days as president of his company, a 65-year-old owner-founder said: "If I stop working, I will die." Hershon interviewed one owner-founder who, when asked about his lack of preparation for a successor, replied: "Why, that would be like putting one foot in the grave."[6] In his study of succession in small businesses, Christensen observed:

> At this point, attention should be called to the reluctance shown by
> many small businessmen toward thinking about the problem of succession.
> By their words and actions, they seem to imply that the subject is a morbid
> one, no more suitable for discussion than an unpleasant physical affliction.
> The unwillingness of many small businessmen to sign a will is another
> symptom of the same point of view.[7]

Some owner-founders view succession as an affirmation of their own
mortality. They may regard appointing a successor as acknowledgement that
the company will continue to exist even though they may die. Samuels, the
66-year-old owner-founder of Home Mortgages, seemed to realize this
relation and refuted it:

> When I was chairman of the board and president, I was involved in the
> every-day running of the business. I won't say I was too old for that, but the
> directors told me and pushed me, saying I can't run a one-man business.

In addition to the above emotional considerations, the owner-founder's
attitude toward the appointment of a president may be influenced by financial
considerations. As an equity holder, the owner-founder will benefit from a
smooth transition to a competent president. Gregg explained the financial
importance of the transition in this manner:

> By 1960, the family had invested $500,000 in the firm. It's a matter of
> preservation of capital. If I hadn't provided for succession, we'd have been
> in the soup. We put in $500,000 back then, and it's worth ten times more
> now. I had to provide for succession so as to preserve the family's
> investment. I knew that if I didn't provide for top-flight management, the
> wealth would disappear. One of the key factors in preserving the business
> is the succession of management.

The board members, the company's bankers, or the investors frequently
emphasize these financial benefits to offset the owner-founder's emotional
resistance to the appointment of a professional president.

The above considerations concern any manager, regardless of his
management style, who is faced with bringing in his replacement. Levinson
refers to similar concerns on the part of any top manager in dealing with his
successor.[8]

The degree of conscious awareness of these emotional and financial
concerns differs among owner-founders. Though most are aware of the
financial reasons, many do not consciously reflect upon the impact of the
emotional issues on their attitude toward succession. Nonetheless, the

emotional aspects do influence an owner-founder's attitude toward the appointment of a president and the role played by the owner-founder in the appointment. The emotional implications of succession usually overshadow its possible financial benefits for most owner-founders. Therefore, the majority of owner-founders ignore or resist succession. Christensen reported that a great number of the more than one hundred presidents of small businesses whom he interviewed did not even mention the question of succession as a problem of major concern.[9] According to the experience of the venture capitalists interviewed, it is a rare exception to find an owner-founder who voluntarily appoints a professional president. Usually, it is the board of directors or the lenders who must initiate the process of appointing a professional president.

ROLE OF THE BOARD OF DIRECTORS
IN THE PRESIDENT'S APPOINTMENT

In order to better understand the board's role in the appointment process, we will look at the board's function in companies managed by an entrepreneurial owner-founder and the changes in the board's role brought on by the companies' growth.

Evolution of the Board of Directors

Most boards of directors do not play an important role in companies managed by entrepreneurial owner-founders with little need for outside financing. Some of these organizations have no boards of directors at all. "When I was going to night school, I was considering having a board and studied the possibility, but I found out I wouldn't know what to do with a board. How would I use them?" replied a president, being interviewed in the first stage of the research, to an inquiry about his company's board. Where there is a board, it is often composed of family members, personal friends of the owner-founder, or the firm's executives. "Prior to this time, the board had existed merely as a legal technicality," states the writer of the case on Desert-Dry Rainwear Corporation, "and had been comprised only of Desert-Dry's principal stockholder, his wife, and 'close friends.' "[10] "Close friends" referred to the major stockholder's brother-in-law, who was an employee of Desert-Dry and was replaced by the owner-founder's personal lawyer. Similarly, Design Associates' Board is composed solely of the firm's executives and the owner-founders.

The composition of such a board of directors enables the owner-founder to dominate the board and limits the board's effectiveness. Family members and close friends may not have the necessary expertise to evaluate and guide the firm. Emotional ties may restrain them from acting contrary to the owner-founder's wishes. Executives, who may possess the required expertise, are restrained by the fact that the person whom they, as board members, are to direct and guide is simultaneously the person who determines their promotions and incomes. As a result, any board primarily composed of such members is frequently dominated by the owner-founder. In *The Board of Directors in Small Corporations*, Myles Mace states:

> It became apparent very early in the inquiry that the typical small corporation board of directors was largely a vestigial legal organ which included merely subservient and docile apointees of the owner-manager. Obviously, such a board did not participate in the management of the business, but it did meet the letter of the law by having certain persons designated as members of the board.[11]

Discussing his role as director of Ford Motor Company in 1926, while the first Henry Ford was president, David Gray testified:

> [I] was a mere figurehead as a Ford director and [my] actions as such were purely perfunctory.... Plans were submitted and voted upon in such a manner as Henry Ford requested. Everything was cut and dried beforehand, and the directors really had no say and no discretion....[12]

The entrepreneurial owner-founder's relations to the board are congruent with his relations to the firm's executives. He dominates the board just as he dominates the organization's executives. He maintains the right to initiate and change the board's decisions in the same manner that he changes and countermands his executives' decisions.

As the business grows, it often develops a need for outside funds to finance its growth. The acceptance of outside financing frequently brings about a change in the board's composition. In some cases, banks require an increase in the company's equity as a prerequisite to lending. Venture capitalists typically demand a seat on the board as a condition for their investment. Selling shares to the public brings other independent members onto the board. Thus, as a firm grows, the composition of the board usually transforms from one whose members are dominated by the owner-founder to one whose members are independent of him. An executive of Control Systems, Alex Smith, described such a change as the result of obtaining venture capital: "That changed the picture from having a board of directors that was fairly tightly held to a board of directors not personally related to John Kelly."

Grego describes the impact of the change in the board's composition on the internal power structure of the board (Figure 10).[13] As the firm develops,

FIGURE 10
Internal Power Structure of the Board

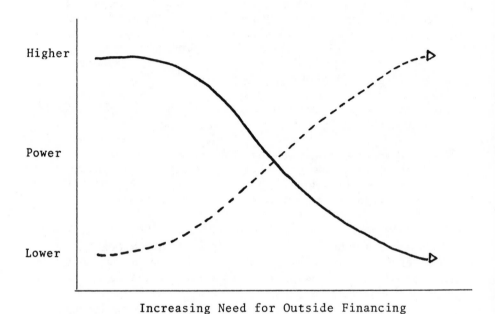

Increasing Need for Outside Financing

--- = Power of Lenders and Investors
—— = Power of Owner-Founder

Source: adapted and used with permission from Jaime Grego, "The Changing Role and Function of the Board of Directors" (D.B.A. dissertation, Harvard University, Graduate School of Business Administration, Boston, 1976).

the owner-founder's relative power decreases and the power of those providing funds increases, according to Grego.

The board's role in the appointment of a professional president depends on the board's assessment of a need for a president and their power to implement their decision. The board's power is a prerequisite for the implementation of decisions contrary to the owner-founder's desires. While the owner-founder is usually a board member himself, in the ensuing discussion, "board member" refers to members other than the owner-founder.

Power of the Board of Directors

In the present study, power is defined as the ability of actor A to modify actor B's behavior.[14] A and B may represent an individual, a group, or an organization. This definition can therefore be used in terms of two individuals, two groups, or a group in relation to an individual, as in the case of the board to the owner-founder.

The board's power vis-à-vis the owner-founder is determined by three factors: the board's financial control of the company; the relationships of the board members to the owner-founder; and the board's evaluation of the importance of the owner-founder's expertise to the firm.

The board may exert financial control over the firm through ownership of equity or control of the firm's loans. The importance of the board's equity position depends not only on the percentage of the equity held by board members, but on the distribution of the remainder of the firm's equity (Table 2). At Control Systems, the board's financial control represented a strong source of power. Although Control Systems' owner-founder, John Kelly, owned 25 percent of the stock, the other 75 percent of the stock was held by NCC and two venture capital firms whose representatives served as the other members of the board. At the other extreme, the financial control of Design Associates' board provided it with very little power relative to that of its owner-founders. The firm's owner-founders owned 60 percent of the firm's equity, and the firm had no outstanding loans.

The relations of the board members to the owner-founder play an important role in the board's power over the owner-founder. The greater the number of board members who are outsiders, the greater the board's power versus the owner-founder's power (Table 3). In this respect, too, Control Systems' board was more powerful than the other boards, since it was completely composed of outside members. Design Associates' board had the least power, since all of its members also served as the firm's executives. Their positions as subordinates to the firm's owner-founders prevented them

TABLE 2

Equity Structure of Companies at Time of Appointment of President

Company	Percentage of Total Equity Held by Owner-Founder	Dispersion of Remainder of Equity
Home Mortgages Company	11[a]	Widely dispersed among public
Control Systems Inc.	25	Held by three firms whose executives were the majority of the board of directors
Design Associates	58	Board members owned 20 percent; other 22 percent dispersed among other executives of firm
Metal Manufacturing Company	12[b]	Board members owned 12 percent; rest widely dispersed

[a]The Samuels family owned 18 percent of the firm's equity.

[b]The Gregg family owned 38 percent of the firm's equity.

Source: Compiled by the author.

from making recommendations or taking action as board members contrary to the owner-founders' wishes.

Family and friendship ties are another aspect of the relationship between the board and the owner-founder that tend to affect—to reduce—the board's power against that of the owner-founder. At Home Mortgages, these ties were a factor that kept the board from appointing a professional president to replace the owner-founder. Three of the members of the board were the owner-founder's relatives, and the outside board members were hesitant to act because of their friendship with Joseph Samuels. One board member stated:

> Joe has a warmth in his relationships that makes it difficult to be dispassionate in your assessment of him. He is a generous man and enjoys sharing his family and personal life with his business colleagues. Over the years, we have developed a mutual friendship.

Referring to hiring a professional president, another board member said: "The banks did what we thought was necessary but were reluctant to do."

The third factor concerning the board's power is its assessment of the

TABLE 3

Composition of the Board of Directors at Time of Appointment of President[a]

Company	Relatives of Owner-Founder	Employees of the Firm	Representatives of Lenders/Investors	Total Number of Members
Control Systems Inc.	0	0	4	4
Home Mortgages Company	3[b]	3	5	8
Metal Manufacturing Company	1	0	7	8
Design Associates	0	9	0	9

[a]All numbers exclude the owner-founder.
[b]All relatives are also full-time employees, and therefore are also counted under "Employees."
Source: Compiled by the author.

importance of the owner-founder's expertise to the company. This depends not only on the necessity of the functions that the owner-founder performs but, more importantly, on whether these functions can be performed by someone else. The owner-founder may be irreplaceable in organizations with innovative products if the owner-founder is the driving force behind the design of these products. This was the case, for instance, with Henry Ford and Edward Land in the early days of Ford's and Polaroid's history. The owner-founder may also be irreplaceable in some service firms where, to a great extent, he is the firm's product. An executive at Design Associates stated: "The clients are used to dealing with Bruce Wallace. To them, he is the firm, so it is hard for them to extricate themselves from Bruce Wallace." As illustrated by the following statements, the board members held similar views on the question of whether anyone could replace Bruce Wallace:

> Our only asset is people, in that this is different from a manufacturing firm. Our greatest asset is Bruce Wallace. He was and is the firm.... The nature of the design business is another factor. It's an ego business. To our clients, Bruce Wallace is Design Associates.
>
> Bruce Wallace is the dominant force in this firm and that will always be the case until we have a very expensive funeral.... If Bruce Wallace would leave tomorrow, I would leave today. If we got to the point that Bruce was not totally involved in marketing, then I would leave. He is the driving force.

To summarize briefly, the Control Systems' board of directors was the board that had the greatest power over the owner-founder. The boards of Home Mortgages and Metal Manufacturing had less, but still sufficient, power to initiate the process of appointing a new president in spite of the owner-founders' resistance. Design Associates had the least powerful board, one that clearly could not take any action against the owner-founders' wishes.

Assessment of the Need for
A Professional President

In situations where the board has sufficient power to overrule the owner-founder, it appoints a new president despite the owner-founder's resistance only after its members have agreed that the owner-founder is ineffective as president and that replacing him is the best alternative open to the firm.

As a rule, a board of directors is extremely hesitant and conservative in judging the owner-founder as incompetent for several reasons. First, it is difficult to assess the owner-founder's competence. Even in a company with severe financial problems, the board must examine whether the problems are of a short- or long-term nature and whether they are due to poor management or to other factors beyond management's control. "We are confused about where [the owner-founder's] abilities begin and end," stated a long-time board member about an owner-founder.

Board members who are investors in, or lenders to, the firm have an added reason for caution in their judgment of the owner-founder's performance. When investors or banks decide to lend money to the firm or to buy its stock, they evaluate the owner-founder's management capabilities and agree to finance the firm only after a favorable assessment of the owner-founder's skills has been made. They are naturally reluctant to reverse their earlier judgments of the owner-founder and are therefore slow to judge him incompetent.

The board's customary initial step toward improvement of the organization's management is to suggest to the owner-founder that he delegate more responsibility to others and be more professional in his management style. At both Home Mortgages and Control Systems, board members initially attempted to improve the company's performance in this way. Another step, sometimes taken by the board, is to encourage the owner-founder to hire or appoint an executive vice president who may eventually become president. At Control Systems, for example, Peter Davis was initially hired as executive vice-president. If such measures do not improve the situation, the board considers appointing a professional manager as president. A board member of Control Systems described the events leading to the appointment of Davis as president in this way:

> Peter Davis was hired to be the executive vice-president. John delegated nothing to Peter. "Peter, the quality control is a mess, go clean it up. Be my errand boy here, be my errand boy there." We were probably close to losing Peter Davis if we had not promoted him to president. We tried to let John make that decision, to give Peter the authority to run the company. He didn't.

Even in cases where the board has sufficient power to appoint a president and has evaluated the owner-founder as being ineffective as president, the board still hesitates to appoint a professional president. The owner-founder, despite his weaknesses, is a known entity, and there is the risk that the new president will be less competent than the owner-founder. As one board member said, "There is nothing more embarrassing than replacing the owner-founder with someone who is even less competent." Secondly, the board is concerned with the negative publicity which may result from a forced succession. Finally, the board is not a single entity, but a group of individuals. Delays may occur because a majority decision is necessary to replace the owner-founder. Often, however, some board members must wait many months before their colleagues are convinced that the owner-founder should be replaced by a new president.

DYNAMICS OF THE APPOINTMENT PROCESS

The appointment of the professional president may be the result of the interaction of several parties: the owner-founder, the board, the investors, the lenders, and the executives. The number of parties that do become involved in the appointment process depends on the owner-founder's willingness to voluntarily appoint a president.

In situations where the owner-founder initiates the appointment, the board is usually the only other party that becomes involved. The owner-founder does consult the board about the appropriateness of such an action and confers with them in choosing the candidate. He, however, has the most decisive role in the process. This was the situation at Metal Manufacturing and at Design Associates.

Lenders, investors, and executives only become involved in initiating the appointment of a professional president in situations of severe crisis where pressure must be put on the owner-founder to appoint a president. Investors usually act through their representatives on the board. This was the case with Control Systems, where the four outside board members represented 75 percent of the firm's equity. Lenders may pressure the owner-founder through their position as board members or, more directly, through threatening to call their loans. In the latter case, the board and the lenders often form a coalition. This occurred at Home Mortgages.

In trying to decide on a course of action, the board often questions the company's executives about the owner-founder's competence. In some companies, the executives have diverse opinions about the owner-founder. In other situations, there may be a severe breakdown in the relationship between the majority of executives and the owner-founder. In the latter case, the executives may encourage the board to replace the owner-founder. In Control Systems, for example, a coalition was formed between the board and some of the executives to replace the owner-founder as president.

Each party's role in the appointment process is reflected in their reasons for the appointment (Table 4). In instances where the owner-founder initiated the appointment, the board's reasons for the appointment reflect its passive stance. This was the case in Metal Manufacturing and Design Associates. The owner-founder's reasons differed from the board's reasons at Home Mortgages and Control Systems, where the president was appointed despite the owner-founder's opposition. The board considered succession necessary to compensate for the owner-founder's management weaknesses. The owner-founders disputed the alleged managerial weaknesses. Samuels explained the firm's financial problems in this way: "The reason why we got into problems was strictly because of expansion and because we were highly leveraged with not enough capital." Owner-founders tend to project the reasons for the company's problems on factors outside their control. Abraham Zaleznik

TABLE 4

Reasons for Appointment of the Professional President

Company	Board of Directors	Owner-Founder(s)	Executives
Home Mortgages Company	To bring in a professional manager as president Samuels close to retirement	Pushed into it by the board and the lenders	Believed owner-founder forced to by the board and the lenders Firm experienced severe financial problems
Control Systems Inc.	Lack of trust in Kelly resultant from many incidents over the years Kelly's management deemed unsuitable for firm Executives threatened to leave	Divergent motivation between equity holders of Control Systems and NCC Under pressure from the board	Perceived owner-founder's management unsuitable for the firm Lack of trust between Kelly and the board
Design Associates	Owner-founders wanted depth of management Needed someone to run day-to-day operations	Wanted to build some redundancy into the system to achieve depth in key areas of management	To give day-to-day operations to the president To manage growth To enable Wallace to go to Washington
Metal Manufacturing Company	Owner-founder wanted it A natural and normal succession to give executive VP title for the job he was doing Executive VP was competent and owner-founder wanted less involvement with the firm	To preserve family's wealth "Proud of Metal Manufacturing and don't want it to disappear" Executive VP was competent and would do well as president Desire to spend more time on community activities	Executive VP was already doing job of president. Just a change in title Owner-founder wanted someone with more professional training as president Owner-founder wanted to spend more time on outside interests

Source: Compiled by the author.

49

observed this to be a prevalent way for the human psyche to deal with failure or disappointment.[15] The divergence between the owner-founder's and the board's reasons indicates the amount of persuasion and/or coercion often required on the part of the board to appoint a president.

DEFINING THE PRESIDENT'S JOB

At all sites except Metal Manufacturing, the owner-founder and the president did not have a detailed discussion of their respective responsibilities during the appointment process. At Metal Manufacturing, according to the employees and the members of the board, Ryan had been performing all the functions of president for three years before his promotion. "It was nothing big," commented one board member, "just a well-deserved change in title." This comment also reflected the reaction of other board members and most executives to Ryan's promotion. Nevertheless, at the time of Ryan's promotion, a board member suggested that Ryan and Gregg discuss their respective responsibilities in detail and write them down on paper. As chairman of the board, Gregg's responsibilities initially included management of stockholder and bank relations and long-range planning. Ryan was responsible for all other functions. This division of responsibility was announced along with Ryan's promotion in the firm's annual report.

At the other three sites, there was little detailed discussion of responsibilities beyond designation of titles (Table 5). At Control Systems, John Kelly retained responsibility for long-range planning and the export market. At Design Associates, the agreement was for Wallace to be responsible for "originating new business, obtaining resources necessary to support the firm, and overall financial controls," with Cooper being responsible for the "day-to-day operations" and the management of relationships with existing clients. At Home Mortgages, the division of responsibility between the owner-founder and the president was not explicitly delineated. "No one really sat down and defined [the division of responsibility] and verbalized it or put it on paper," stated a board member. "The understanding was: 'Yeah, we'll run it together. You [the president] are in charge of daily things, but when you make a big decision, I want you to keep me informed.'" Another board member said:

> I thought that Steve was brought in as chief executive officer.... I cannot recall whether there was a discussion as to Joe's role. We did agree that he would spend four months, at least, on vacation. That was our common assumption. Not much was said about Joe's and Steve's division of responsibility. My understanding was that Joe's role would be something between a figurehead and the guy that runs the day-to-day operations.

TABLE 5
Titles of Owner-Founders and Professional Presidents

Company	Owner-Founder's Title	Professional President's Title
Design Associates	Chairman of the board and chief executive officer	President and chief operating officer
Metal Manufacturing Company	Chairman of the board	President and chief executive officer
Control Systems Inc.	Chairman of the board	President (no c.e.o. designated)
Home Mortgages Company	Chairman of the board and chief executive officer	President and chief operating officer

Source: Compiled by the author.

> That's what I thought Joe was striving for.... We were vague in our instructions to Joe regarding his responsibility and what we thought his role ought to be.

INITIAL REACTIONS

The intensity of the reaction to the appointment of the professional president is a function of the degree of change brought on by the appointment. When asked about their reaction to Ryan's promotion to president, the executives at Metal Manufacturing responded:

> It was overdue if anything. He should have been made president earlier.
> It didn't make much difference to us, to be truthful. We knew that it was going to come, and I can't say that it was a surprise.
> Though it was a change in title, it seemed to me that he had been functioning as president for some time prior to his appointment.

Gregg and the board members interviewed also made comments similar to the ones above. At Metal Manufacturing, the reaction to the appointment was very mild because it actually made very little difference to the responsibilities or relationships of the executives, the president, and the owner-founder.

The discussion below describes companies where the president's appointment was perceived as actually producing change in the executives' relationships and responsibilities.

Initial Reaction of the Executives

When an outsider is hired as president, the new president is naturally a matter of great interest to the executives. Who is this man to whom they will be reporting? Many executives "try to find out about him" by investigating his "track record"—what his prior jobs were, under what circumstances he is leaving his present job, and what his co-workers' or employees' opinions of him are. They develop evaluations of the new president on the basis of data gathered from these investigations: "I had a negative appraisal of him," "He seemed like an okay guy," "He was a big zero," or "He seemed okay—we saw a list of companies he had been at, and they looked good." Thus, many executives form opinions of the person who will become president before he even assumes his new post.

In addition to curiosity about the president, the executives may react to his appointment in three ways: with optimism, as representing an opportunity; with apprehension; and with resentment. An individual executive may feel a combination of these emotions at the same time. For example, one executive at Control Systems resented the new president because he had replaced the owner-founder but, at the same time, recognized that the change in management might well offer an opportunity for his own advancement. Another executive at Control Systems also saw the appointment of the new president as a possible opportunity for personal advancement. He was, however, also apprehensive about whether his skills would be satisfactory to the new president.

Many executives, especially in firms where a crisis precedes the change in presidency, consider the appointment of the new president as an opportunity for themselves and for the company. "My position was defined and fixed by Kelly. This was not so with the new president. So, it was an opportunity to change things for the better," said one executive. The appointment of the new president may also be seen as an opportunity for introducing professional management into an organization managed by an entrepreneurial owner-founder. Some executives may also view the succession favorably because it may decrease nepotism or family control in the firm. Finally, some executives look forward to the arrival of the new president because they hope to use him and his role as a buffer between themselves and a too demanding owner-founder. "Bruce is like Captain Bligh of the 'Bounty,' and Bill [the president] could've become Fletcher Christian," commented an executive of Design Associates. "The executives would've welcomed somebody who could have helped them do their jobs and protect them from Bruce."

The appointment of the new president may cause anxiety and apprehension for some executives. "I took an attitude of 'What changes is he going to make? What kind of man is he going to be?' Everyone came to me and told me everything would be the same, but I still wondered." The degree of "tremble, fear, and wondering," as one executive described it, depends on the executives' perception of the president's power. At Control Systems, many executives were concerned about losing their jobs under the new president. At Home Mortgages, however, where most of the executives still considered the owner-founder to be more powerful than the president, no one voiced any concern about job security under the new management. Since personality factors such as insecurity or low self-confidence also influence an individual's reactions in these situations, it is not at all unusual to have equally competent and successful executives react to the incoming president with very different degrees of apprehension.

Many executives used the word "resentment" in describing their first reaction to the new president. Most executives who felt they had been "passed up" for promotion resented the president. The following conversation, which exemplifies the above reaction, took place with an executive at Design Associates:

> My feeling was that the president should have been someone from the inside. Me, for example. When I was at my last job, I managed [X dollar amount] of sales and [X number of] people.
> Q.: What if someone from inside had been promoted but it had been someone other than you?
>
> A.: I think it would've been fair.... No, now that I think of it, I was the only one ready for the job.
>
> Q.: But what if someone else [from inside] had become president?
>
> A.: I would've been mad as hell. I would've torn him up.

Other members of this firm stated that two other executives within the company had considered themselves potential candidates for the presidency. A board member explained that one reason for the choice of an outside president had been the owner-founder's fear that the selection of any one of these three contenders as president would have caused the other two to leave the firm. Another of the three contenders commented:

> Promotion from inside wouldn't have worked. No one was competent enough in everyone's eyes to handle it. If it had been an insider, it would've been more bitter. The jealousy and resentment would've been greater.

Two other causes for resentment toward the president were sympathy for the owner-founder and jealousy of the new president's salary or employment contract. "My attitude," said an executive at Control Systems, "was one of resentment. I was attached to Kelly." Such executives were sympathetic to the owner-founder because he had "his firm taken away from him." At both Home Mortgages and Design Associates, the presidents had employment contracts considered as lucrative by many executives. Statements such as the following were made by executives at these two companies:

> I envy the guy. He is making great money. He walked himself into a good position. There was some resentment towards him when he came in. Because of his salary, I believe.

During the initial period of the new president's tenure, company executives closely scrutinize his actions and performance. In this way, they evaluate the validity of their own earlier assessment of his potential impact on their careers. At Control Systems, Peter Davis was aware of the scrutiny:

> You'd be amazed how they watch you. You are the only one viewing them, but there are a hundred people watching you. They see what functions you ask about if you visit them. They see if you are interested in them. They want to know how much you know about their area of responsibility.... It's like being in a fish bowl.

Hodgson, Levinson, and Zaleznik observed the same behavior on the part of the staff members toward the new superintendent at the hospital they studied. They observed that,

> Not even the simplest of personal habits or administrative actions were exempted from microscopic examination and interpretations that were palpably apprehensive and critical.[16]

Initial Reaction of the Owner-Founder

The amount of change that is caused by the appointment of the new president is one determinant of the initial reaction of the owner-founder. Since David Ryan at Metal Manufacturing had had most of the responsibilities and the authority of the president for several years prior to his promotion to president, his relationship with Thomas Gregg, the owner-founder, was well established by the time he was appointed president. Therefore, Gregg's and Ryan's reactions to the appointment were minimal.

At the other firms, however, the appointment of the president had considerable impact on the owner-founders. They were concerned with establishing a working relationship with the new president and determining the effect of his appointment on their own relationships with the company's executives.

If an outsider is appointed as president, developing a working relationship requires the owner-founder and the president to learn about each other's skills, personality, and management style. Building a working relationship also requires the owner-founder and president to determine each other's responsibilities. The difficulties of delegating and dividing responsibilities greatly increase if the president and the owner-founder have only minimally discussed the division of responsibilities prior to the president's appointment.

Entrepreneurial owner-founders have more difficulty than professional ones in resolving the result of the appointment for themselves and for their role in the organization. Their ambivalence is reflected in contradictory statements or in the contradiction between their talk and their actions. Executives at several sites made observations similar to the following one, articulated by an executive at Design Associates:

> For the longest time, Bruce would come to us and say, "You work for Bill [the president] and make him a success. You push him and help him." But Bruce wasn't letting go.
>
> Q.: He was saying one thing and doing another?
>
> A.: I've known Bruce a long time, and he's a great talker. He was just talking. Bill would make a decision, then Bruce would say to Bill in front of me and others, "Goddamn it, Bill, I don't run this firm that way." Also, Bill would make a decision, and it would be reversed by Bruce.

The entrepreneurial owner-founders were also ambivalent about their relations to the firms' executives. On the one hand, they acknowledged to themselves that the executives must formally report to the new presidents. On the other hand, they still found it difficult to break the behavior pattern set by long years of direct involvement in the company's operating decisions. They still, at least partly, expected the executives to report to them.

At all sites, except Metal Manufacturing, the relations of the owner-founder to both the executives and the new president were in a state of flux three months after the president's appointment.

Initial Reaction of the President

The president hired from outside is at a distinct disadvantage compared to the insider promoted to president. The insider is acquainted with the firm's business, procedures, and personnel. The outsider must learn about the firm's policies and procedures while he is managing the firm. Referring to the time when he was brought in from the outside to serve as the president of a firm called Empire Manufacturers, Peter Davis described the initial period of his presidency in this way:

> I was trying to find out what was going on in the company. I tried to determine what information was available and how to obtain it.... As the new president, you also think about questions such as "How many executives can work with you? How competent are they? Whom are you going to keep? How are you going to keep them?" You have to decide all this while you're working with the executives and managing the company.

During the first few months at his new post, the president attempts to establish relationships with several groups other than the executives (Figure 11). If the owner-founder has maintained a post in the firm, the president tries to build a working relationship with the owner-founder. The president also learns about the board members and their expectations and method of operation. Lastly, he is usually concerned with several groups outside the firm. The banks, the investors, suppliers, and clients evaluate the president and his potential impact on the firm. As one president stated, "Outsiders look and ask: 'Is the company strong? Will the directors support the president? Will the company be sold?' Outsiders watch with care."

Initially, two management tasks face the president. The first is to minimize the disruptive impact of the management transition on the firm's personnel and operations. The second task is to solve any urgent problems facing the firm. This is especially important in situations where the president's appointment was provoked by a crisis. He must solve the crisis first. Only at a later stage can he address its cause.

The president then faces a particularly difficult task at this early stage of his appointment. He is learning while managing. He is being scrutinized by many audiences. Lastly, the audiences often have conflicting expectations of what his role should be. The board, the analysts, and the banks may see the president as an agent of change, while the owner-founder may view him as a number two man who will bring very little change to the company.

During the first three months or so, the president, the owner-founder, and the executives are learning about and evaluating each other. Even with an insider being appointed president, managers attempt to assess the impact of the changes in titles of the president and the owner-founder on the relationships in the firm. Furthermore, during this time, they develop tentative expectations and assessment of each other that may be solidified or changed with the passage of time.

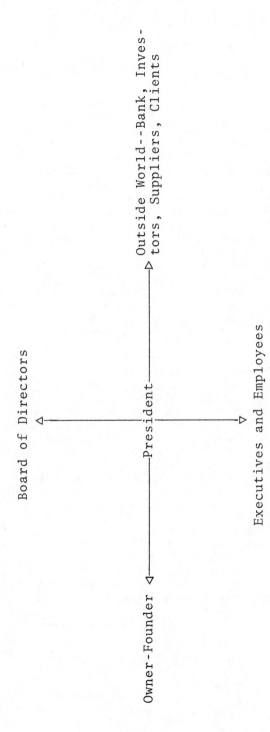

FIGURE 11

Relations Managed by the Professional President

Board of Directors

President

Owner-Founder

Executives and Employees

Outside World--Bank, Investors, Suppliers, Clients

Source: Constructed by the author.

57

NOTES

1. Eleanor Carruth, "Sweat + Leverage = $200 Million for Arthur Cohen," *Fortune*, December 1975, p.108.

2. David C. McClelland, *The Achieving Society* (New York: Free Press, 1961).

3. Harry Levinson, "Conflicts That Plague Family Businesses," *Harvard Business Review* (March–April 1971): 91.

4. Ibid.

5. Elisabeth Kübler-Ross, *On Death and Dying* (New York: Macmillan, 1969), pp. 2, 4.

6. Simon A. Hershon, "The Problems of Management Succession in Family Businesses (D.B.A. dissertation, Harvard University, Graduate School of Business Administration, 1976), chap. 4, p. 9.

7. C. Roland Christensen, *Management Succession in Small and Growing Enterprises* (Boston: Division of Research, Harvard University, Graduate School of Business Administration, 1953), p. 15.

8. Harry Levinson, "Don't Choose Your Own Successor," *Harvard Business Review* (November–December 1974): 53–62.

9. Christensen, *Management Succession*, p. 15.

10. "Desert-Dry Rainwear Corporation (A)1" (Boston, Massachusetts: Intercollegiate Case Clearing House, #4-676-011, (c) 1975), p. 4.

11. Myles Mace, *The Board of Directors in Small Corporations* (Boston: Division of Research, Harvard University, Graduate School of Business Administration, 1948), p. 87.

12. Anne Jardim, *The First Henry Ford: A Study in Personality and Business Leadership* (Cambridge: MIT Press, 1970), p. 81.

13. Jaime Grego, "The Changing Role and Function of the Board of Directors," (D.B.A. dissertation, Harvard University, Graduate School of Business Administration, 1976).

14. For definitions and typologies of power, see Chester I. Barnard, *The Functions of the Executive* (Cambridge: Harvard University Press, 1938), pp. 172–73; David V. Bell, *Power, Influence and Authority* (New York: Oxford University Press, 1975), especially chaps. 1 and 2; R.A. Dahl, "The Concept of Power," *Behavioral Science* 2 (1962): 201–15; Richard Emerson, "Power Dependence Relations," *American Sociological Review* 1 (February 1972): 31–41; John R. P. French and Bertram Raven, "The Bases of Social Power, in *Studies in Social Power*, ed. Dorwin Cartwright (Ann Arbor: University of Michigan Press, 1959), pp. 150–67; D. J. Hickson et al., "A Strategic Contingencies' Theory of Intra-Orgainzational Power," 16 *The Administrative Science Quarterly* 2 (June 1971): 216–29; David Mechanic, "Sources of Power of Lower Participants in Complex Organizations," 7 *American Science Quarterly* 3 (December 1962): 349–64; J. Thibaut and H. H. Kelly, *The Social Psychology of Groups* (New York: John Wiley & Sons, 1959), especially pp. 120–23.

15. Abraham Zaleznik, "Management Disappointment," *Harvard Business Review* (November–December 1967): 59–70, especially 65–67.

16. Richard C. Hodgson, Daniel J. Levinson, and Abraham Zaleznik, *The Executive Role Constellation: An Analysis of Personality and Role Relations in Management* (Boston: Division of Research, Harvard University, Graduate School of Business Administration, 1965), p. 254.

4

IMPACT OF SUCCESSION
ON MANAGEMENT RELATIONS

Succession usually results in disturbances in the ongoing relations in the firm and necessitates establishing new relations or revising old ones. The chapter just concluded addressed the relations between the owner-founder, the president, and the executives during approximately the first three months of the president's appointment. The present chapter discusses subsequent developments in these relationships.

METAL MANUFACTURING COMPANY

At Metal Manufacturing, Thomas Gregg, the owner-founder, and David Ryan, its chief executive officer, mutually agreed on their division of responsibility. The functions of the two men were complementary. Gregg was responsible for stockholder and bank relations; Ryan had authority over all of the firm's operations and reported directly to the board. While Gregg's duties emphasized the firm's interface with the outside environment, Ryan's responsibilities focused on the internal affairs of Metal Manufacturing. Both men found the division of responsibility satisfactory since it reflected each man's personal interests.

The two men's personalities also complemented each other well. Ryan was perceived as the "all-business, hard-nosed" type, while Gregg was thought of as the more lenient, paternalistic person. Ryan made the following statement:

> Now Thomas can go around as the paternal founder, the nice guy. Everyone calls him Tom. It's a role he likes. He can walk around the plant and can be nice to everyone. As Daniel Gregg [board member] said to me, "You'll be the SOB, and he'll be the nice guy."

Ryan and Gregg had an excellent relationship. The following comment was made by a director:

> Tom and Dave have very complementary roles. They both perform better with the other being there than they would if the other were absent. They both respect each other and learn from each other.

Gregg had high regard for Ryan's management capabilities as executive vice-president:

> After Dave was here for five years, he was getting itchy. He makes a plan for everything. He told me he had gotten to a point where he had to make a decision as to whether he should stay or not. I said, did making him president fulfill his life plan? He said, "Yes." I said, "Okay, you're president." I was glad to give him the responsibility.

Gregg judged Ryan to be a competent president.

> Dave has amazing dedication and determination. He is an absolutely dedicated man to achieving his goals.... He definitely knew all the things that needed to be done. He can put things in and see that they are done.

The two men rarely disagreed. The executives saw Gregg as supportive of Ryan, and the board members interviewed knew of no disagreements between them. Ryan regarded Gregg as a valuable consultant. He stated:

> Thomas Gregg's and my relationship has always been good. It's good to have someone to bounce things off of once in a while. Though I don't take everything to him or go to him continuously. But on anything important, we can talk back and forth. This is good for me and helps keep him informed.

CONTROL SYSTEMS INC.

At Control Systems, Davis was hired with the understanding that he would serve as the firm's executive vice-president. Kelly, however, never recognized this appointment. According to the company's executives, Kelly was extremely reluctant to delegate responsibility to Davis. He reprimanded executives for consulting with Davis and reversed decisions made by Davis.

After Davis had been at Control Systems for four months, the board appointed him as president and Kelly as chairman of the board. Given the history of repeated disagreements with the board, Kelly suspected that his tenure as chairman might be a temporary one. During his five months as chairman, he was very concerned about increasing the size and liquidity of his equity holdings in Control Systems. Kelly also spent some time developing a long-term plan for the company. As president, Davis reported directly to the board and was responsible for the firm's operations.

At best, the relationship between Kelly and Davis was strained. The two men never established a harmonious working relationship. Kelly and Davis were concerned about each other's intentions and motivations, and each questioned the other's ability to perform his duties.

DESIGN ASSOCIATES

At Design Associates, Wallace had carefully planned for the first months of Cooper's tenure as president. The plan was for Wallace and Cooper to work together for two months, during which time Cooper would become acquainted with the firm and its employees. Then Wallace would go to Washington, D.C., for three months to serve as a full-time consultant to the United States government on a special task force. During this time, Cooper would assume full responsibility for the firm's existing accounts and establish his role as the firm's president. When Wallace returned from Washington, he would assume his new role as the firm's chairman and chief operating officer and would focus on "originating new business, obtaining the resources necessary to support the firm, and overall financial controls."

Except for Wallace's three-month absence, the above plan was never realized. When Wallace departed for Washington, the executives thought that he had left

> no clear mandate as to who was running the business except Cooper's title. Wallace was on the phone every day, and all of us knew that Bruce was running the firm, and Bill was executing his orders.

When Wallace returned, he saw that Cooper had not assumed a leadership position in the firm. Furthermore, several of his top executives told Wallace that Cooper had failed to win the confidence of the firm's larger clients and, moreover, that some of them did not even want to deal with him. Wallace felt that he had tried to delegate responsibility to Cooper, but Cooper had not

> come up to our expectations.... Too often, a situation is one where you have to say, "Come on! Let's get up and do it." He does not have the

perception to say, "Here is what needs to be done and what we should do." Rather, he wants to be told what to do.

Cooper's views of the competence he had displayed at Design Associates differed considerably from Wallace's. A year and a half after his appointment, he stated:

> At this point, there is nobody in the organization who doesn't know I can get clients and solve problems.... We [Wallace and himself] can both close business and get new business. When he is here, he does that, and I move into the operating side of the business. That's necessary.... In terms of new business, Bruce is super, and I am good at it.

He felt that Wallace had circumvented his authority and had not given him the necessary power for carrying out his responsibilities.

> He [Wallace] can't even visualize letting go.... The basic problem is that it is hard for him to give up authority. When Bruce went away, that was highly evident. He called all the time. He wanted to maintain direct involvement in internal operations even when he was in Washington.
> While Bruce was away, I did a good job of managing the firm and added 10% of our revenue on the book.... He came back with the idea that he needed to be personally involved in all areas. In the process of doing this, he went directly to the senior people about getting reports of their activities, as opposed to getting the reports from me. This by-passing did cause me to lose ground in terms of internal relations and coordinating my activities with Bruce.

Cooper recognized that he and Wallace had not reached an agreement about their respective roles in the firm. He believed, however, that with some communication, they could come to an agreement on their actual division of responsibility.

The relationship between Wallace and Cooper was very different from those between the owner-founders and presidents at the other sites. In spite of his disappointment, Cooper expressed understanding of Wallace's desire to have personal, immediate access to the functional supervisors who officially reported to the president. Referring to Wallace's actions, Cooper stated:

> This is Bruce's style of management. He's always been highly involved in the firm's operations, and he derives personal satisfaction from directly working with the executives....

At the same time, he acquiesced to Wallace's behavior.

If the president says, "Everyone must report to me and everyone must come through me," saying "This is my football and that is your basketball," it's nonsense. That way, a great asset [reference to Wallace] is lost from the clients and the customers. Some things have to be resolved and talked out—which accounts will you take and which accounts will I take. He has to become more involved in client relations and move down some. All does not need to go through me. I want him with me. For example, we get an in-house consultant, and the guy wants to work with Bruce, that's beautiful. It's simple. We can have a box either to me or around me. The key thing is to get the most leverage out of Bruce. . . . The division of responsibility should be based on each man's interests and skills rather than formal titles.

As evidenced by the above statement, Cooper had great respect for Wallace's abilities and saw his role as a complementary one to Wallace's.

Bruce is terrific. While he was away, he got two important clients for us. All this, while he was in Washington. . . . My position is to be a solid number two, not a challenging number one. So, I operate with a different heaviness of hand. I'm demanding, but I come in with . . . less heavy a bang.

A year and a half after Cooper's appointment, Wallace's behavior toward him had also been void of confrontation. He felt guilty about uprooting Cooper from his previous job, yet he did not feel that Cooper was sufficiently competent to assume the responsibilities originally intended for him.

HOME MORTGAGES COMPANY

As at Design Associates, the owner-founder at Home Mortgages kept the titles of chief executive officer and chairman of the board, and Madanick assumed the title of president and chief operating officer. The owner-founder's view of the relationship between himself and the president differed considerably from the president's.

Samuels, the owner-founder of Home Mortgages, believed that in the first six months he

gave Madanick a free hand. I bent over backwards for him. He felt he could do it his way and prove himself. In the beginning, when we discussed something, I would say, "It's entirely up to you, you're the president."

Madanick's appointment had run one year when Samuels decided that this arrangement was not working out. Despite his claims that he wanted to give

Madanick a free hand, he felt that Madanick was making decisions without adequately consulting him and that some of these decisions had hurt the firm financially—although Samuels acknowledged that the amounts were insignificant.

Madanick, the president, was convinced that his own treatment of Barry Stein, Samuels' relative who had been the firm's previous president, was the main determinant of Samuels' attitude toward him.

> My security and my meeting the favor of Mr. Samuels depend solely on my pushing the abilities of Barry Stein. I had every intention of pushing and developing his abilities, when I joined the company, but now, I have doubts about how much can be done. I talked to Mr. Samuels about this when I got employed, and we thought maybe Barry could become executive vice president and then president, and I would become chairman of the Board. This hasn't worked out based on Barry's abilities, not my lack of desire because it would be to my advantage to do so.

Furthermore, Madanick assessed the number of times that Samuels and he had disagreed on major business decisions as "insignificant." He believed that "other than Mr. Samuels' personal or family problems, we would not have any problems."

Samuels and Madanick had conflicting personalities and management styles. Samuels was an informal, down-to-earth man with a high school diploma; Madanick was more formal and aloof and a college graduate. Samuels was an entrepreneurial manager, while Madanick had a professional style of management. This difference in styles caused considerable friction between the two men. Samuels perceived Madanick as being too formal and not sufficiently involved with the firm's daily operations. Madanick, on the other hand, felt that Samuels did not delegate enough responsibility to executives, became too involved in insignificant details, and relied too much on emotions and intuition rather than on logic or analysis in making decisions. Their criticism of each other grew as time went on.

OWNER-FOUNDER'S RELATIONS TO PRESIDENT

The relationship between the owner-founder and the president in the four companies ranged from harmonious ones with great mutual respect to bitter ones with mutual criticism. The owner-founders' attitudes toward the presidents were influenced by their own personal attributes as well as by the attitudes shown by boards of directors and the owner-founders' families.

Impact of Personal Attributes

Most owner-founders have a high need for controlling the activities and decisions in the firm. In his study of entrepreneurs, Kets de Vries stated:

> The entrepreneur is easily threatened and unable to work in a subordinate relationship since that would imply a repetition of the childhood frustrations which he is desperately trying to overcome. His need for autonomy and dominance and achievement are outcomes of the reaction formation to the fear of weakness caused by his anxieties.[1]

This need for control influences most owner-founders' business relationships. It underlies their delegation contracts with their subordinates while they were presidents—and thus influences directly all decisions that are of interest to them—and it also underlies their domination of the boards for as long as such control is possible. Finally, it prevents them from delegating decision making to their presidents and prompts them to review any decisions made by their presidents and to reverse them if they are not to their liking. An executive described an owner-founder's control over a president in this manner:

> The president does what the owner-founder tells him. The owner-founder runs the company.... He tells the president to 'stand in back of me,' and the president does it. He tells him to sit, and he sits. It's the owner-founder's company, and he runs it.

Fear of no longer being indispensable to the firm prevents some owner-founders from delegating authority to the presidents and impels them to belittle the presidents' accomplishments. One executive made the following comment regarding a decision made at one company:

> That decision used to be made by the owner-founder. But with the new president here, it was the president who decided, not the owner-founder. Therefore, from his point of view, if the decision is wrong, it's the president's decision. If the decision is right, then it's because that's the way we've always done business around here.

Most owner-founders wish to have the firm managed by the president in the same management style they have used themselves. At Metal Manufacturing, Gregg's professional management style facilitated his endorsement of Ryan's professional management style. At the other companies, however, the owner-founders had an entrepreneurial style, and this divergence in styles was a major reason for the poor relationships between the owner-founders and their presidents at these sites. A board member at one firm suggested: "Obviously, their styles are different. No matter what the results, he [the owner-founder] couldn't be happy with the approach."

Effects of Other Groups

The owner-founder's relatives can affect the owner-founder's relationship with the president significantly. The Gregg family's influence is an example of a family's positive impact on the relations between owner-founder and president. Thomas Gregg was the only family member who was a full-time employee of Metal Manufacturing. Two of his brothers were affiliated with the company, one as a board member and the other as a part-time consultant. Both were amply qualified for their duties. The family shared Thomas Gregg's belief that a smooth transition to a professional president was necessary for the preservation of their wealth. They agreed with Thomas Gregg's assessment of Ryan's competency and commended Thomas Gregg for the smooth succession. Daniel Gregg, who was a board member observed:

> I think this [Ryan's succession to the presidency] was a natural evolution and, it must be said, in part a tribute to my brother whose temperament is such that he puts more emphasis on making things work than worrying about how he would look.

In other cases, the owner-founder's family may aggravate the relations between the owner-founder and the president. At some companies, many family members are full-time employees, and they benefit from various formal and informal privileges because of this family status. Since the continuation of such privileges is often jeopardized by the professional president, the family members are likely to see the professional president as a threat. Consequently, they attempt to undermine him. In some situations, the owner-founder's relations with the president are influenced by the president's handling of the owner-founder's relatives. According to Madanick, this was the case at Home Mortgages. Moreover, family members often solicit the owner-founder's support in any arguments or disagreements with the president. Thus, the president's disagreements with family members often turn into disagreements with the owner-founder, providing him with additional reasons for hostility toward the president.

The members of the board, too, can have conflicting influences on the owner-founder. Each board member encourages the owner-founder to establish the kind of relationship with the president that will be most beneficial from that board member's personal viewpoint. Some inside board members allow their actions as board members to be determined by what is beneficial to them as the firm's executives. The same is sometimes true of family members on the board. Their feelings as family members determine their actions as board members. Those outside board members who have no personal interest usually encourage the owner-founder to build a harmonious working relationship with the president. Their direct efforts to help establish such a relationship increase in proportion to the disagreements between the owner-founder and the president. At Metal Manufacturing, where the outside board members knew of no disagreements between the owner-founder and the president, they had a grateful but largely passive stance toward this relationship. At Home Mortgages, one year after Madanick's appointment, by which time the disagreements between Samuels and Madanick had become more bitter and less reconcilable, the outside board members began to take an increasingly active role in attempting to mediate and resolve these disagreements.

Resolution of Divergent Influences

The previously discussed personal attributes and group pressures often have disturbing influences on the owner-founders. As a result, many owner-founders face a conscious or subconscious dilemma regarding their relations with their presidents. On the one hand, they realize that they should delegate decision making to the presidents and form working relationships with them to achieve a smooth succession. The owner-founders and their families will benefit financially from such a transition. The outside board members and, in some cases, the owner-founders' relatives may also encourage them to develop positive working relationships with the presidents.

At the same time, other considerations, as discussed above, act to deter the owner-founder from establishing a harmonious relationship. He may feel that he knows the substance of the business better than the president does. The president may make decisions that will hurt the firm. He may be irritating the owner-founder's family and threatening their job security and privileges. The owner-founder may not agree with the president's management style. Finally, the president's success may mean the displacement of the owner-founder as the central figure in the firm.

The owner-founder's particular relations to the president are shaped by the matter of whether and how the two figures resolve the dilemma facing them. The transition did not pose as much of a dilemma to Thomas Gregg as it did to the owner-founders at the other sites. Gregg was accustomed to managing the firm jointly, since he had done so in the days before his father's death in 1966. Gregg and his family agreed with Ryan's management style and trusted his competence. Gregg further saw the transition to Ryan's presidency as an opportunity for himself to fulfill his desire of working on community affairs. Regarding his reaction to giving up control, he conceded:

> I simply had an emotional problem. I brought this thing along in the last twenty years and was used to controlling it. But that's not right. You have to bring in young people. I knew that, if I brought in a president, I would no longer have control. But if I didn't, the company would be out of control. I decided to bring in a president. Anyway, I have more fun now.

An executive at Metal Manufacturing summed up Gregg's resolution of the dilemma he faced:

> Tom tried hard to give up the reins rapidly. He recognized that he couldn't have it both ways. He hired the man [Ryan] for a reason and felt that he had to follow through. From Tom's point of view, the faster he gave Dave control, the better, when Dave was appointed president. There was no doubt that Dave was really running the company. You received the impression that Tom would support Dave's decisions, even if Tom personally did not agree with them, unless he felt that the decision was morally wrong.

This dilemma led other owner-founders to contradictory behavior during the first year of the president's tenure. Many executives at Home Mortgages and Design Associates made remarks similar to the following one by a Design Associates executive:

> The executives know that Bruce has not yet given up the responsibility. Bruce says, "Don't talk to me, talk to Bill," but he doesn't mean it. They go to Bill, and if they don't like what he says, they go to Bruce. So, why go to Bill in the first place?

By the end of the first year of the presidents' tenure, Bruce Wallace and Joseph Samuels had resolved the dilemma facing them by consciously deciding to take over responsibilities originally intended to be their presidents'. These owner-founders used their evaluations of the presidents as lacking sufficient competence to justify their decisions. They were reluctant to admit that other considerations may have influenced their decisions. Observers such as members of the boards or executives, however, referred to the owner-founders' personal attributes, the divergence in management styles, and the influence of different groups in explaining the owner-founders' behavior.

PRESIDENT'S RELATIONS TO OWNER-FOUNDER

Like the owner-founder, the president is subject to diverse pressures. The outside members of the board of directors usually view the president as an agent of change, expecting him to bring professional management to the firm. Different groups of executives often have conflicting expectations regarding the president's role in the firm. Some executives hope that he will bring changes to the firm's management, while others want him to preserve the status quo.

The owner-founders also have expectations about the presidents' accomplishments. Some owner-founders, Thomas Gregg, for one, welcome the changes implemented by the presidents. Many others, however, are not certain of their precise expectations in regard to the president. They have some thoughts about professionalizing management or about having the presidents reduce their work load, but they have not translated these objectives into specific actions.

These anticipations, nevertheless, put the president into a position where he must bring the opposing expectations into balance. It is often impossible to satisfy all the demands made of him, and inevitably, some party will be angered by whatever course of action he takes.

At Metal Manufacturing, Gregg delegated decision making to Ryan. Their duties complemented one another's and were built on each man's respective strength and interest. At sites where the owner-founder had an entrepreneurial management style, however, he and the president did not agree on each man's role. Their relationships were marked by frustration and misunderstanding.

The presidents' perceptions of their relationships with the owner-founders often differ radically from the owner-founders' views. The presidents often misinterpret the owner-founders' attitudes towards them; they usually perceive these attitudes to be more favorable than they really are. At the time Samuels was making negative statements about Madanick's competence, Madanick believed that Samuels was "satisfied that I have the ability and capability of running Home Mortgages." Cooper had a similar misconception of Wallace's evaluation of him.

In firms where the entrepreneurial owner-founder remains associated with the business after the president's appointment, he frequently does not allow the president enough freedom and authority for effective management. Eventually, the president begins to feel frustrated and overcontrolled. He feels that the owner-founder's constant review of his decisions, coupled with the owner-founder's tendency to go around him, make him incapable of effective performance as president.

Presidents faced with the above situations attempt to establish a working relationship with the owner-founders by discussing their viewpoints with them. The differences between owner-founders' and presidents' views of a proper division of responsibility, however, are often too great to be resolved by talking. Madanick, president of Home Mortgages, described Samuels' job in this way: "He would like a place that he can come to and discuss odds and ends and feel secure that the company is running well." His view was quite different from Samuels' idea of his role. In essence, Samuels pictured himself as the principal decision maker in the firm. He considered Madanick's role to be that of implementing Samuels' decisions according to Samuels' directions. Cooper and Wallace had similarly divergent views of each other's roles.

Once the president realizes that he and the owner-founder cannot agree on a mutually satisfactory division of responsibility, he must choose one of two strategies. One strategy is to confront the owner-founder. Madanick chose this strategy: at a board meeting, Madanick stated that he could not operate effectively as president because of Samuels' usurpation of his authority and decision-making prerogatives. Thus, by officially involving the board, he invited an open confrontation between Samuels and himself.

The second strategy for the president is to be passive. Cooper at Design Associates chose this strategy. He seemed willing to accept any division of responsibility established by Wallace.

> I'd love to have Morse and Adams report to Bruce on professional things and report to me on administrative things and budgetwise. It would be fine if we did that. The box [the organization box representing the president's post] is just a tool. He could work with some clients and I would work with others.

Cooper subsequently backed his words by action and surrendered most of the areas of responsibility, formally the president's, without much resistance.

EXECUTIVES' RELATIONS TO PRESIDENT

In the initial period after the president's appointment, most executives have conflicting emotions about the president and are concerned about the president's impact on their careers and relationships. About a year after the president's appointment, most executives have established a relationship with him that is internally consistent with their assessment of his competence and his impact on their careers.

Negative Attitudes

Jealousy is a major cause of hostility toward the president. The executives who feel that they were passed up for the presidency expect the president to prove that he is more worthy of becoming the president than they are. No matter what the president accomplishes, the slighted executive still thinks that his accomplishments as president would have been more significant. To justify such feelings, the executive becomes anxious to prove that the president is not sufficiently competent for the post. An individual at Design Associates described the executives' reaction to the president: "He made a mistake when he first got here. And all said, 'Aha! That's one mark against you.' It's as though they were waiting for him to make a mistake." If the president is fired or demoted, the slighted executive will have a second chance to be appointed to the presidency. This wish that the demotion occur motivates the executives to undermine the president by degrading his accomplishments before their peers and subordinates and by magnifying his mistakes.

The president's salary and other compensation are further causes for jealousy. The following statements were made by one executive at Design Associates and one at Home Mortgages:

> There is some resentment. Everyone knows that the president is using a lot of the company's resources. With his salary and his car and expense account. There is some resentment that the money that is used for that could be used otherwise.
>
> As far as I'm concerned, no one is worth that much money [reference to the president's salary].

The executives' fear of loss of power or perhaps their actual loss of power as a consequence of the president's decisions causes dislike of, and apprehension towards, the president. Executives were concerned over loss of power and privilege only in firms where they perceived the president as having the power to influence their careers or salaries. At all the sites, the presidents had a more professional management style than the owner-founder. Some executives, especially long-time employees under the owner-founder, were anxious about losing power in the firm as a result of the new president's management. They feared being demoted or fired because of lack of necessary skills and style of management. When the president did demote or fire an executive, the other executives' fears of similar measures against them seemed only to magnify their distrust and anger towards the new president.

Some executives were also concerned about the loss of a more subtle kind of power—the informal power and privileges they possessed by virtue of their personal relationships with the owner-founder. One manager, who had been the owner-founder's confidant, described the impact of the new president thus:

> John had problems in finance, service, and accounting. I was privy to the information about what was going on with these areas, but I was not on

> the firing line.... When Peter became president, I got isolation. Now, I'm not privy to any information. But [the president's appointment] didn't affect my actual day-to-day operations.... In areas not directly related to my job, I'm not at all considered, I believe.... Now, I just exist here.... I'm resigned... I'm in a corner. No one bothers me. My influence in the company has gone down considerably.

The executives' assessment of the president's competence is consistent with their emotional attitude toward him and his impact on their power in the firm. In one firm, all executives interviewed except one had a generally positive relationship with the president, and they rated him as competent. The exception was an executive who had suffered severe loss of power as a result of the president's appointment. His negative comments regarding the president's competence, although at great variance with the other evaluations, were consistent with his anger over his loss of power.

The ability of the executives to act on the basis of their negative emotions depends to a large extent on the owner-founder's support of the president. The executives carefully scrutinize the words and actions of both owner-founder and president to determine the owner-founder's support of the president. If the executives realize that they cannot secure the owner-founder's support either because he refuses it or because he has left the firm, the dissatisfied executives pursue one of three courses of action. The first is to leave the firm of their own accord. The second is to stay at the firm, refuse to cooperate fully with the president, and criticize him continuously; this course of action usually leads to involuntary separation from the firm. Finally, some executives stay and eventually transform their attitude of frustration or resistance to one of resignation.

> I used to be very frustrated about my job and position and the direction in which the company is going because it's wrong. But that gives you ulcers.... I can't worry about that. If I get my job done, that's enough. I only worry about my job. No one asks my opinion, and I don't give it. It's less frustrating that way.

If the executives sense that it is possible to convince the owner-founder to officially demote or dismiss the president, they try to persuade him to do so. Most of the executives interviewed at Design Associates felt negatively towards Cooper. Individually, they tried to persuade Wallace to demote or fire Cooper. Wallace felt this pressure: "I've had a tremendous amount of pressure from many people here to admit that I made a mistake." However, Wallace refused to fire Cooper or demote him. The executives were frustrated by Wallace's refusal but nevertheless continued their efforts at persuasion.

Positive Attitudes

Those executives who see themselves as benefiting from the president's appointment have a positive attitude toward the president. Some executives are pleased by the new president because they prefer to work with his more professional management style rather than the owner-founder's entrepreneurial style. At one site, a manager described his views this way:

> Peter does things more by mechanics and prediction. There is less reaction and more planned work.... I't like a stone has been lifted off your neck.... With Peter, we're concentrating on things that are happening now and, at the same time, on a parallel path, are planning for six months from now.... With John Kelly, you'd go your merry way, and in January, you'd be dealing with January problems, and in February, with February problems, and so on. Now, we're planning ahead. This costs more money, but it allows us to manage better.

At Home Mortgages, a board member stated:

> Certain people felt that there were better leadership and better communications with Steve than with Joe Samuels. Joe does not believe in meetings, and if there are meetings, they are one-sided. The decision filters down from the top since Joe dominates the meeting.

Other executives support the president because they prefer their personal relationships with the president to their relationships with the owner-founder. At Control Systems, an executive explained:

> John Kelly was not very enlightened in trying to motivate people. He'd yell at you in front of others. He was demeaning. His interpersonal relationships were terrible. People were constantly yelling back and forth at each other. It's alright to be yelled at when the guy is right, but when he's irrational, it's terrible.... John was a loner. He was secretive. Peter is more open. You know where he's going and what his thinking is.... Peter is very helpful. He's willing to help you.

Executives who have a positive attitude toward the president usually have high regard for the president's competence and believe that he has a positive impact on the firm. The following remark, made by an executive who liked Madanick personally, contrasts dramatically with another executive's evaluation of Madanick as a "big zero."

> Steve [Madanick, president of Home Mortgages] has done things for the company. For example, moving Howard to become the general mer-

chandising manager was a great move. He has been good for the company.... Madanick has done other things, too. First, the banks like him.
Secondly, the vendors like him. He gives the company an aura of pro-
fessionalism, and they like it. Apparently, the trade journals like him....
We have been getting a lot of good articles from the trade journals since he
became president.

The owner-founder's relations with the president determine what actions
the executives take on the basis of their own positive attitude to the president.
When the owner-founder has a positive relationship with the president, the
executives openly voice their support and defer to the president. Where the
owner-founder does not support the president, the executives' actions depend
on the president's power vis-à-vis the owner-founder's. If the president is
clearly more powerful, the owner-founder's lack of support is disregarded.
This circumstance occurred at Control Systems. Though the owner-founder
did not support the president, most executives considered the owner-
founder's remaining time with the firm to be limited. This fact in addition to
their dislike of the owner-founder resulted in open support of the president by
most of the executives. Referring to the firm's employees, an executive
reflected: "I never saw one hundred and thirty people get behind one man so
quickly." Where the executives recognize the president and the owner-
founder as equally powerful and the owner-founder is critical of the president, the executives try not to align themselves with either party. Although
in private conversations they may commend the president's performance,
they refrain from revealing their support for the president to the owner-
founder.

PRESIDENT'S RELATIONS TO EXECUTIVES

After a year's time, the presidents had made their own evaluation
regarding the top executives. The presidents' attitude to each executive could
usually be correlated with the presidents' perception of the executive's
attitude toward them.

The presidents showed different degrees of skill in identifying the
executives' relations to them. Cooper seriously misunderstood the executives' assessment of his competence. On the other hand, Davis could describe
each of the top executive's goals and motivations with great accuracy.

The actions that a president could take, based on his attitude toward a
particular executive, depended on his power in the firm. If he had little power,
he could not fire or promote any executive without the owner-founder's
approval. His ability to act independently was severely checked by the
owner-founder's involvement. In such cases, the president's only alternative
was to attempt to change the negative attitude toward him without, or with

limited, recourse to rewards or punishments. If a reversal of sentiment did not occur, the president suffered not only the executives' hostility but humiliation resulting from his inability to act.

Where the president is more powerful than the owner-founder or has his support, he can deal with the executives' displays of negative attitudes toward him in several ways. He can replace them with executives who will cooperate with him, or he can demote them and place other people in the higher posts. Such actions by presidents are extremely common.

CONCLUSION

This chapter has addressed the issue of the relationships between the owner-founder and the president and between the executives and the president (Figure 12, part A). Implicit in the discussion has been the impact of the owner-founder's relations with the firm's executives on the other relationships in the firm (Figure 12, part B).

If the owner-founder supports the president, he delegates authority and responsibility to the president. The president then has the opportunity to demonstrate his managerial ability to the executives. Furthermore, the owner-founder's support of the president allows the president to gain power over the executives. If executives do cooperate with and support the president, he can reward them with promotions and increased salaries. If they dislike the president and do not cooperate with him, the president can demote or fire them. The owner-founder's support of the president encourages the executives to have a positive relationship with the president.

Supporting the president requires the owner-founder to realign his relationships with the company's executives to reflect the new reporting relationships. He must stop working directly with the executives on the firm's operating matters; rather he must work largely through the president. In many cases, the owner-founder resists making these required changes in his relationships with the executives. He derives personal satisfaction from his relationships with the executives and from being involved in the company's operating decisions. Samuels repeatedly referred to his daily chats with executives two or three levels below the president as an integral part of his role as the firm's chairman of the board. He stated that no matter who the president was, he himself would never stop "kibbitzing with the boys."

Some executives discourage the owner-founder from changing his relationships with them. Sometimes they are anxious to work directly with the owner-founder, since they feel that it is he who has the authority and makes the final decisions. An executive at Design Associates made these comments:

> Who do people work for? Bruce. Who hired them? Bruce. Who is

FIGURE 12
Management Relationships

A

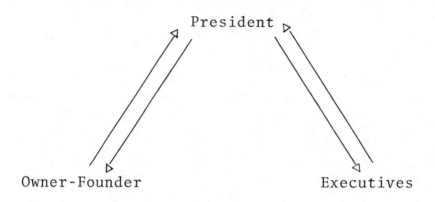

B

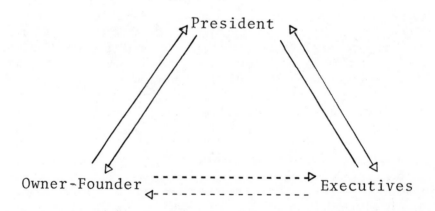

Source: Constructed by the author.

successful? Where does the money come from? Who rewards them? So, they perform for Bruce. The loyalty goes around the president to Bruce. Presidents come and go. Bruce is here to stay.

Other executives resist altering their relationships with the owner-founder becaue they derive psychological satisfaction from these relationships. These executives view the president as an intruder into their relations with the owner-founder. As one executive said, "It's like being a stepmother. Here, the father and his children have a good relationship, and you are brought in as a stepmother."

When the relationship between the owner-founder and the executives is not realigned to conform with the new president's role and formal authority, the president's authority is undermined by the owner-founder. He and the executives continuously go around the president, making it difficult for him to perform effectively. Moreover, the owner-founder and the executives reinforce each other's actions. The executives point to the owner-founder's lack of support for the president as their reason for not respecting the president's authority:

> Bill Cooper is a titular president. There was no passage of power and authority or respect. And there won't be, and there doesn't need to be. There is absolutely no need.

The owner-founder, in turn, points to the executives' attitudes as proof of the president's incompetence and the necessity for his circumvention of the president's responsibility.

The owner-founder who remains associated with the firm often plays an important role in the president's success in the firm. If he supports the president, the president will have the opportunity to obtain sufficient power to manage the firm and gain the executives' support. When the owner-founder does not delegate to the president and largely maintains his former relationships with the executives, the danger that the president will fail is greatly increased.

NOTE

1. Manfred F. R. Kets de Vries, "The Entrepreneur as Catalyst of Economic and Cultural Change: A Psycho-Entrepreneurial Approach" (D.B.A. dissertation, Harvard University, Graduate School of Business Administration, 1970), p. 162.

5

FINAL OUTCOME

Of the four companies studied in depth, at only one did the president and the owner-founder both remain affiliated with the company and develop a harmonious working relationship. This ratio of one in four is not representative of the incidence of successful transitions in the larger business community. Interviews with venture capitalists and other experts in regard to these successions indicated that the actual incidence of successful transitions is less than 25 percent. However, those people interviewed did not agree on the exact occurrence of such transitions.

METAL MANUFACTURING COMPANY

At Metal Manufacturing, the relationship between Gregg and Ryan has continued to be good. Gregg and the other board members are fully satisfied with Ryan's performance. The division of responsibility remains agreeable to both owner-founder and president. In the minds of the firm's executives, there is no question about Ryan's final responsibility and full authority over the company's operations.

CONTROL SYSTEMS INC.

During the months that John Kelly was chairman of Control Systems' board, the relationship between him and the other board members became increasingly acrimonious. The disagreements between them were now so frequent that the board members decided to dissolve the position of chairman of the board and to terminate Kelly's salary. Kelly continued to serve as a board member, but a few months later, according to Kelly,

> they said, "We think it would be a good idea for you to make a more complete separation from Control Systems. Maybe you're not being productive to your investment or to [those of] others' if you stay." Since it had gotten to the point that I could not even get anyone on the Board to second my motions for discussion of problems, I decided to resign as a Board member.

After resigning from Control Systems' board of directors, Kelly acquired a smaller firm in Maine which manufactures valves. He vows, "I will never involve my company with venture capitalists again."

Peter Davis remains Control Systems' president, and Harris, the major partner of NCC with the largest ownership in Control Systems, serves as chairman of the board. Since Kelly's resignation, the rate of increase in the company's sales has declined, but its profitability has risen as compared to the average rate of profitability during Kelly's presidency. According to most executives, executive morale has improved considerably.

HOME MORTGAGES COMPANY

In August, approximately one year after the president's appointment, Samuels decided to take control of decisions which normally fell within the president's domain. Samuels explained:

> I gave Madanick six months to run things and saw that it didn't work out. I had to take over. I had to. If I had a different man as president, maybe it would've made a difference.

Madanick, on the other hand, felt that he had been "leaning over backwards for a year" in his relationship with Samuels and that he had attempted as much as possible to cooperate with Samuels. But by December, he felt he could no longer tolerate the situation. "Frankly, I've had it up to here," he said, raising his hand to his throat. He continued:

> Samuels has been usurping more and more authority and has just taken over. I can't bend to him any more. I've bent back as much as possible. I've been on vacation and have thought about this a lot. I have to call it to a head because things can't go on like this for much longer. Why be frustrated all the time? Why go home like that?... Put yourself in my

place. I can't stay on with this kind of a situation. Joe has taken control, and it's not good for me or for the other managers to continue like this.

Madanick felt that Samuels was undermining him and making it impossible for him to function as chief operating officer. He cited Samuels' employment of Jerry Sullivan as a top executive of Home Mortgages without consulting Madanick as the most recent incident of Samuels' efforts to undermine his authority. Madanick also saw Samuels' decision to raise a lower level employee's salary without consulting the two employees' superiors as yet another indication of Samuels' unwillingness to operate within the formal chain of command. Madanick claimed, "Joe is reaching for the jugular vein if he can get it. I don't know how to play that game and don't care to learn."

Throughout this period, Madanick and Samuels each had informal meetings with individual outside board members in which they discussed their view of their relationships with each other. The frequency of such meetings increased when Madanick decided that he could no longer tolerate the situation and had to bring things to a head.

According to one director, Madanick stated at the January meeting of the board of directors that he would like to discuss "the fact that Jerry Sullivan was hired without Madanick having been consulted." An argument then ensued between Samuels and Madanick as to whether Madanick had actually been consulted. At the end of the meeting, the board suggested that Samuels and Madanick work together and improve their relationship. The board's understanding was that it would take several months for this to be accomplished and that the process would require more active involvement of the outside board members in the relationship. The board meeting ended with the outside members hopeful about future improvements here.

The day after the board meeting, Samuels, without conferring with the outside board members, asked Madanick for his resignation. In the following two weeks, numerous meetings took place; many of them were between outside board members only, and some of the meetings included either Samuels or Madanick. The final result of the meeting was that 21 days after its January meeting, the board asked Madanick for his resignation. The remainder of Madanick's employment contract was bought by Home Mortgages and Madanick vacated his office one month after the board meeting.

After Madanick's resignation, Samuels described his future plans thus:

> I will hire a new man [as president] and do what I wanted to do from the beginning, which is to go into semi-retirement. I will spend the winters in Florida and be up here for eight months of the year. I will come in and talk with the president to know what's going on. I'll have coffee with the boys downstairs [executives five levels below the chairman of the board on

the organization chart] .... In the meantime, while I'm choosing a new president, I'll run the company. Why not? I've been doing it for the past thirty years, and I'm good at it, so why not?

A search committee was established by the board to hire a new president. Five months after Madanick's resignation, a new president had still not been employed. Samuels was acting as the firm's chief operating officer in addition to serving as chief executive officer and chairman of the board.

DESIGN ASSOCIATES

One year and six months after Cooper's appointment as president, Wallace asked Cooper to seek employment elsewhere. At the same time, it was made known to the top executives, through word of mouth, that Cooper's duties were restricted to managing a new division that had been established within the firm to design lobbies of large office buildings and banks. However, Cooper retained his title as president. Though there were no announcements made or memoranda written, all the top executives were aware that they should formally report to Bruce Wallace as they had done before Cooper's employment. "The farce is over" and "we've given up the charade" were some of the comments made by the top executives.

Wallace did not wish to fire Cooper for two reasons. First, he was concerned about the repercussions of such action on the firm's reputation.

> This is not like a manufacturing company where, if the president does not work out, the family can take him and hide him. We're in the people business. We're well known in this industry. All are watching to see what's happening. We're visible. If you raise your eyebrows, the competitors know. Plus, we have clients. If you say to them, "We've made a mistake," then they'll say "What's happening?" You say, "In all honesty, it didn't work out." "Why?" The more you explain, the more questions you raise.

Secondly, he was concerned with the impact of such action on Cooper's future. He felt that he had uprooted Cooper from his previous job and so hesitated in cutting adrift a man more than fifty years old.

After a few months of searching, Cooper had been unable to obtain satisfactory employment elsewhere. Wallace then presented him with a second option: remaining at the firm with a reduced salary with responsibility for Design Associates' new division. At the end of the field work, Cooper had not yet decided whether to take this option. His primary endeavor was to avoid confrontation. Cooper's status in the firm was described in this way by one executive:

> He's like a wounded elephant wandering around the herd. It's sad. It's
> better to kill him off. He's become a professional eunuch.... Bill has never
> met...[a new client who had increased the firm's revenues by 30 percent].
> He was not invited to our meetings with them. Have you heard of death by
> exposure? Well, this is death by lack of exposure.

OVERVIEW OF FRAMEWORK

Why did it happen? This is the question the owner-founders, the
executives, the presidents, and the board members often asked themselves in
companies where the transition had failed. From their comments, it was
evident that they had spent some time thinking about this question as well as
discussing it with other managers. The specific question most often raised by
these managers was whether the transition's failure was due to the personal
characteristics of the president or to factors beyond any president's control.

A successful transition from the owner-founder to a professional president depends on the amount of power gained by the president. Power is
defined as the ability of A to modify B's behavior. A and B may represent an
individual, a group, or an organization. At both Metal Manufacturing and
Control Systems, where the transition was successful, the president had a
substantial amount of power. In situations where the president had little
power, however, the transition was a failure. Home Mortgages and Design
Associates are examples of unsuccessful transitions. Therefore, a discussion
of the ultimate result of the succession process must involve an appraisal of
the president's ability to gain power.

Along with deriving it from his position, the new president can gain
power from four sources: coalition with the board; coalition with the owner-
founder; coalition with outside investors and lenders; and his personal
characteristics—his competence and personality.

The question asked by managers, "Was the situation a no-win situation
regardless of who became the president?" focuses exclusively on the first
three sources of power. The question assesses the power available to a new
president from coalition with the company's owner-founder, board, or
financial supporters (investors not represented on the board or in the banks).
The power available to a new president from these coalitions is called
potential power (Figure 13). A no-win situation is when the potential power
is so low that no president, regardless of his personal characteristics, can
make sufficient gains to succeed as president. Any person assuming the
president's post in such a circumstance is doomed to failure.

FIGURE 13
Potential Power

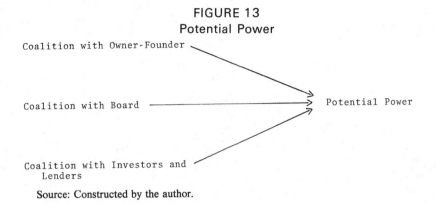

Source: Constructed by the author.

Realized power is the actual power gained by the president during his tenure. How much of the potential power is realized depends on the personal characteristics of the president. For example, if the board and the owner-founder support the employment of a new president to manage the firm, the potential power is sufficiently high, and the president therefore has a chance for success. Once appointed, however, the president may make poor management decisions that anger the board and the owner-founder, and they will withhold their support from him. In that case, the president's realized power will be lower than the potential power initially available to him.

The president's personal characteristics can be viewed as the catalyst that converts potential power into realized power (Figure 14). In a no-win situation, the potential power is so low that, regardless of the president's characteristics, his realized power will be so low as to insure his failure. In "possible-win" situations, the potential power is sufficiently high to give the president a chance for success. The actual outcome depends on how much of the potential power is converted into realized power, given the president's characteristics.

POTENTIAL POWER

The above discussion of the different amounts of potential power implies that power can be measured. The paucity of literature attempting precise measurement of power testifies to the difficulty of this task. The above framework, however, does not attempt to measure power in specific units. Rather, it delineates two categories, into one of which the potential power in a given firm falls: the no-win or the possible-win range. In no-win situations,

FIGURE 14

Conversion of Potential Power into Realized Power

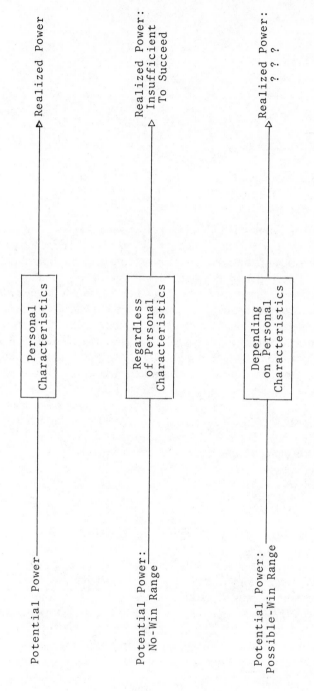

Source: Constructed by the author.

the potential power simply falls in the no-win range. In the possible-win situation, the president's personal characteristics do act to determine his fate. The greater the potential power, the greater the probability of the new president's success.

In situations where the president or the owner-founder was asked to resign, managers who tried to determine whether the president had a chance of success to begin with implicitly used the concept of potential power. They viewed potential power as falling into the no-win or possible-win range. For example, the following comments were made by executives at Design Associates:

> No one could have handled the job [of being president].
> I personally told Bruce to be very careful in doing this thing [appointing a president]. I did not want to be the president just then. I think that if he had asked me to become president I wouldn't have. It's a no-win proposition.

Although precise measurement of power is difficult, the breakdown of potential power into the above categories is operational, as evidenced by the above statements and by other statements in the remainder of this chapter.

Potential power focuses on the willingness and ability of the owner-founder, the board, or outside financial supporters to form a coalition with the new president. The definition of potential power disregards the personal characteristics of the individual appointed as president. Thus, potential power is determined by the factors that influence the propensity of these parties to support a new president through coalition formation with him.

Coalition Between Owner-Founder and President

The owner-founder's coalition with the president is beneficial to the president in many respects. First, the owner-founder provides the president with legitimacy in the eyes of the executives. The importance of this legitimacy is illustrated by the following question asked by an executive at Design Associates with regard to Bill Cooper, its president: "Why should we support him when his support from the top has been cut?" Secondly, by delegating responsibility to the president, the owner-founder gives the president the opportunity to make decisions and exercise his capabilities as president. Lastly, when such a coalition exists, the owner-founder supports the president's decisions and provides him with the information to make effective decisions.

The potential power from coalition with the owner-founder is determined by the owner-founder's dependence on the president, the owner-founder's personal attributes, and his management style.

The more the owner-founder perceives himself as being faced with a problem that only the president can solve, the more motivated he is to form a coalition with the president.[1] Such motivation definitely played a role in both Thomas Gregg's and Joseph Samuels' attitudes toward the presidents of their firms. Gregg hired Ryan as executive vice president with the understanding that Ryan could become president in five years because Gregg believed that he needed "an experienced disciplined professional man... a top manufacturing guy" to manage the firm. He believed that the firm needed a president who had more manufacturing expertise than he himself to solve the firm's manufacturing problems. Gregg also needed a new president so that he could devote more of his own time to community activities.

Home Mortgages had experienced severe financial difficulties prior to Madanick's appointment as president. At the time of Madanick's employment, Samuels was under pressure from the board and the banks to appoint a professional president and, as he described it, "to make sure that I gave him a free hand and that I didn't run the business, because if I did, then he couldn't run the company." Samuels was, therefore, initially motivated to work with Madanick. As time passed, Home Mortgages began to perform well financially, and the pressure from the banks on Samuels subsided. Moreover, Samuels became increasingly convinced that the firm's financial problems had been caused by industry trends rather than by the company's management. He regained his self-confidence and became more and more critical of Madanick's actions.

At the time of the new presidents' appointment, Bruce Wallace and John Kelly perceived themselves as having less need of the new presidents than the above two owner-founders. Therefore, dependence on the presidents did not serve as a motivation for Wallace and Kelly to form coalitions with the presidents. Wallace's firm was performing well financially at the time of Cooper's appointment. Wallace's reason for hiring a president was "to build some redundancy into the system so that we could have depth of management in key areas of business which have to do with the account and overall company problems." The firm could have hired many men other than Cooper as president. Kelly, the owner-founder of Control Systems, did not perceive himself as being dependent on Peter Davis, the president. Davis' appointment was initiated by the board and, according to some executives, forced on Kelly. These executives described Kelly's relations with Davis in terms of hostility and rivalry rather than of dependency.

Personal attributes influence the owner-founder's willingness to form a coalition with the president. The personal attributes of particular importance here are those identified in the last chapter as affecting the owner-founder's relationship with the president. The owner-founder's need for control, his jealousy of the president, his fear of being displaced and of becoming dispensable can be so acute as to preclude his support of any president. This lack of support is usually accompanied by an unwillingness to delegate to the president. The executives at Design Associates, for example, attributed major importance to such factors in the failure of Bill Cooper:

> When I've been in a position to take over responsibility, I've had to fight for it, and there will be a fight to get responsibility from Bruce. Though Bruce says he would like to relieve himself of responsibility, he wouldn't like to.
>
> Bruce wasn't ready to relinquish. He was calling from Washington at six in the morning and waking me up at home. He was flying to New York on weekends. He was not ready to relinquish.

Some officers at Home Mortgages believed that Samuels' personality traits would have prevented his support of any president.

> Q. So you're saying that, if the president is different from the owner-founder, then they have problems. And if they are alike, they will have problems, too?
>
> A. If they are alike, it's worse. There would be a strong personality conflict if they are alike. There was no way, no way of anyone coming in here and making a success of it. I don't care who he was.

The owner-founder's management style is another factor that determines his willingness to form a coalition with the president. An entrepreneurial owner-founder is more likely to refrain from delegating to the president and more likely to undermine the president's authority. He reserves the right to make decisions that are formally within the president's domain because of his longtime habit, when president, of making decisions that impinged upon the executives' authority. Finally, the entrepreneurial owner-founder tends to see the divergence between the president's style and his own as evidence of the president's incompetence.

In the case of many owner-founders, and especially those with an entrepreneurial style of management, their personal attributes and management styles preclude them from forming a coalition with a president, no matter how competent he is. It follows that the potential power from such coalitions is usually in the no-win range. This was the assessment by two executives at Design Associates of the situation in their firm.

> Bruce did not set priorities with Bill. He didn't. Whether Bill could have taken it or not, I don't know. Bruce did not let him sink or swim. He did not have a chance. I don't know if he would have taken it.
>
> No one can succeed in that slot. Bruce Wallace circumvents Bill Cooper continuously. It's impossible to have two masters in one firm. He

does not go through Bill Cooper. Bruce Wallace cannot let go and assume that everything is going well. He has worked hard all his life. He works Sunday mornings and until 2 A.M. many nights. Everyone here is expected to put in more than forty hours per week. Bruce Wallace will not turn the company over to him. He wants to be involved. He's young. He does not want to be in a situation where he is making decisions through Bill Cooper. Bruce Wallace is not the kind of guy who will ever retire. If, at some point,he is forced to walk out of the company, it will be because of his health. Probably, arrangements with him would be where he would be gone for three months and here nine months. He will never walk out of here and go to Florida and retire there. If he does, he will die in two years after the minute he walks out of here.

Bruce Wallace's experience with Morris Palando further confirms the fact that the potential power from a coalition with Bruce Wallace was in the no-win range. Two years prior to hiring Cooper, Wallace employed Morris Palando to serve as the firm's executive vice president. In the opinion of those executives who knew him, Palando was a competent man. One executive described him:

> Morris Palando was very handsome, debonair, and intelligent. He was excellent with clients. He was also a tough negotiator. He was everything you could ask for. He aspired to be the chief executive officer of a company. And he has become one.... Morris came into a situation where rather than Morris leading the situation, he saw Bruce leading the troops. And he saw no change coming, no light at the end of the tunnel—five years, eight years, I don't think he could sit back. He lasted four to five months.
>
> He could not be an understudy. "Morris, watch how I handle this one." He had to lead. Maybe if he had been given responsibility for some clients and Bruce had said, "Morris, you take care of these, and I'll take care of these others," it would have worked.... They [Wallace and Palando] had a healthy respect for each other. Morris could not sit back and see the master perform.

One of the firm's executives recounted Palando's reason for leaving the firm as being "Bruce was taking up too much oxygen."

If a president does stay in such a situation, the relationship between the owner-founder and the president eventually can be described only as a vicious circle (Figure 15). The owner-founder does not give the president adequate support to perform his duties as president. He does not delegate authority to him. He reserves the right to make decisions officially falling into the president's area of responsibility and to reverse the president's decisions. This makes the executives skeptical of the president's authority and reluctant to cooperate with him. Under the circumstances, the president, regardless of his personal characteristics, cannot perform well. His poor performance is in

FIGURE 15
Vicious Circle in Relationship Between Owner-Founder and President

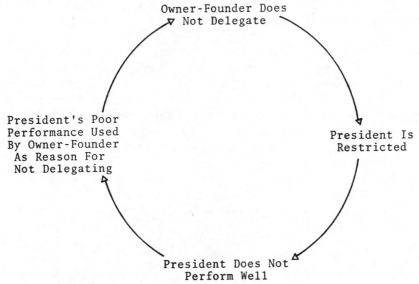

Source: Constructed by the author.

turn used by the owner-founder to justify not delegating to the president. This president is doomed to failure unless he can use the board of directors for support.

Coalition Between Board of Directors and President

The second source of potential power for the president is coalition with the board of directors. The president approaches the board, and the board considers this coalition only after there have been severe disagreements between the owner-founder and the board—as was the case at Control Systems—or between the owner-founder and the president—as was the case at Home Mortgages. As with the potential power resulting from the coalition between the owner-founder and the president, this potential power falls in a certain range. The main concern is to determine whether it falls in or out of the no-win range.

Two questions must be asked: Does the board have enough power vis-à-vis the owner-founder for its coalition with the president to influence the owner-founder? How does the board decide if it should support the president?

If the board's power vis-à-vis the owner-founder's power is so little that it cannot influence the situation, the potential power from the president's coalition with the board is in the no-win range. As stated in Chapter 3, the board's power is determined by several factors, the most important being the board's control over the firm's equity or liquidity. The second factor is the board's composition: the greater the number of inside board members or outside members who rely on the owner-founder for income, such as consulting or lawyer's fees, the less power will the board have over the owner-founder. Also, familial and emotional ties between the board members and the owner-founder can reduce the board members' power. Finally, the board's power vis-à-vis that of the owner-founder is reduced in direct relation to the necessity of the owner-founder's expertise to the firm as well as the firm's capability of providing a substitute for him.

When the board's power is so low that, even with a coalition with the president, this power will be less than the owner-founder's, the probability that the board will form a coalition against the owner-founder is very low. Caplow's conclusion in his study of triads confirms this statement.[2] According to Caplow, two members of a triad will not form a coalition against a third if their combined power is less than the third member's power. If such a situation exists within a firm, the potential power from a coalition between the president and the board is in the no-win range, regardless of the president's competence or the board's assessment of the situation. This was the case at Design Associates, where all board members were also the firm's executives and owned 20 percent of the total stock as compared to the 58 percent owned by the owner-founders. The only tool available to board members is persuasion—indeed a very frail tool in situations of conflict between the owner-founder and the president.

If the board has sufficient power over the owner-founder to make a coalition with the president a possibility, the board is in a position to provide the president with its support. The potential power from such a coalition is determined by two factors. When the board forms a coalition with the president with the aim of firing the owner-founder, the impact of such a dismissal on the company's stockholders, customers, and suppliers determines the potential power available to the president from coalition with the board. The second factor that influences the board is its concern with a smooth succession to professional management. This concern motivates the board to support the president, since his firing may be seen by the executives as a reversion to full control by the owner-founder. In addition, dismissing the president makes the executives cynical about the next president's tenure. The following comments were made by executives at Home Mortgages following Madanick's departure:

> With the next president, there will be a company pool [to bet on the length of his tenure]. I personally want both his ears and his tail when he

leaves.... With somebody coming in, it won't work. People are going to wonder how long he is going to last. He won't command the support of middle or upper management. No one will ally themselves with him.

The next president will be a problem, too. We will be taking bets on how long he'll stay before he comes in. Two months, three months, three months and two weeks, four months, or what? It's Joe's company, and he runs it.

The impact on the executives of firing the president was a main concern of Home Mortgage's outside board members in deciding whether to support Samuels or Madanick.

The potential power from the president's coalition with the board is in the no-win range in companies where the board does not have the necessary power to support the president or in companies where the board has the power to fire the president but is restrained from doing so by the considerations discussed above.

Coalition Between Outside Financial Supporters and President

The last source of potential power for the president is coalition with the company's outside financial supporters—investors and lenders not represented on the board. Large investors usually hold a seat on the board, although this does not seem to be the case with most of a company's lenders. However, if the firm has a major investor not on the board or lenders with significant impact on the firm's finances, it is possible for either of these parties to have enough power vis-à-vis the owner-founder and/or the board to be an independent source of support for the president. As in the case of the board, the outside financial supporters' power is influenced by the probabilities of replacing the owner-founder's expertise.

Since the main interest of outside financial supporters in the company is financial, they usually will not become involved in the conflict between the owner-founder and the president unless the company falls severely short of meeting its financial goals and the cause seems to lie in the firm's management. Even in such cases, outside financial supporters prefer to rely on the board of directors to act, if one exists.

In the unusual situation where financial supporters do become involved to the point of considering a show of support for the president, their decision is made by determining what is most beneficial to their financial objectives. The long-term investors may be precluded from supporting the president by the same considerations as the board: the impact of firing the owner-founder on the other stockholders, the customers, and the suppliers; the impact on the organization's image of stability; and concern with ensuring the replacement of the owner-founder.

In instances where the potential power from the coalition with the board, the owner-founder, and the outside financial supporters is in the no-win range, any president is doomed to failure. The owner-founder will not support him, and the others will not come to his rescue. When the potential power falls in the possible-win range, then the president's personal characteristics do influence the final outcome of the succession.

PERSONAL CHARACTERISTICS OF PRESIDENT

The optimum effect a president's personal characteristics can have is to enable him to convert all the potential power available at a company to realized power. The discussion below addresses situations where the potential power is in the possible-win range, since personal characteristics are irrelevant to the president's fate in the no-win range.

An important aspect of the president's personal characteristics is the matter of his competence. Competence is defined as the effective performance of one's duties. It is usually difficult to develop a consensus about the president's competence because of the disagreements as to what is effective and what his duties are. Moreover, competence is relative to a given situation—an individual may be competent in one job but incompetent in another. This may have been the case with Bill Cooper, the president of Design Associates, who, according to one executive, "left gold dust behind" wherever he had been prior to his employment at Design Associates. But at Design Associates, most executives interviewed were critical of his performance.

Business competence can be divided into two facets: knowledge about the industry one is engaged in—be it textiles, mortgage banking, or electronics—and administrative ability. Administrative ability entails the appropriate use of organization structure, information systems as well as planning, and measurement and reward systems in order to fulfill the company's objectives.

In judging the president's competence, the entrepreneurial owner-founders tended to focus on the president's substantive knowledge rather than on his administrative abilities. This was especially the case with Joseph Samuels. Secondly, the entrepreneurial owner-founder often criticized the president's administrative ability because of the divergence between their management styles. Many of Samuels' criticisms of Madanick stemmed from the fact that Madanick did not manage in the same manner as Samuels.

Another important dimension of the president's personal characteristics is his ability to build positive interpersonal relationships with others. Developing such relationships is ordinarily correlated with being considered competent as a manager, but this is not always the case. As one executive remarked about one president,

> He is a weak leader. He makes no decisions. Personality-wise, he is
> perfect. He's a real gentleman. He's very well liked. As a president, I have
> no respect for him. As a person or a friend, he's one of the finest I have met
> in my life. You have to separate the two.

Building positive relationships entails what John Gabarro identifies as
"development of trust, influence, and expectation" with the owner-founder,
board members, and executives.[3] A prerequisite for building such relationships is knowledge of the firm's norms as well as of each individual's
personality characteristics. In situations where the owner-founder is powerful, the most important relationship to develop is that with the owner-founder,
since this relationship influences the executives' and the board's relationships
with the president as well.

The executives' judgment of the president's interpersonal characteristics
often results from comparing the president with the owner-founder. All
executives interviewed compared the two men. This tendency is particularly
evident in these comments:

> Being the manager and the guy under Bruce [Wallace] is like being a
> Hun under Attila. That's one of the problems. And the whole company
> suffers. Whatever they do, Bruce can do better.

> Bruce, is tough, demanding, and brilliant. Bill is not tough, he is not
> demanding, he is not brilliant. He has none of the above characteristics.

This tendency was noted by Hodgson, Levinson, and Zaleznik in their
observation of management succession. They state that the employees'
reaction to a successor is "not simply to the new man as such, but to
the predecessor-successor pair."[4] The more the president's management
style differs from the owner-founder's, the more he is criticized by the
executives sympathetic to the owner-founder. The president, being brought
into a company under directions from the board to professionalize the
company's management, is bound to alienate both these executives and the
entrepreneurial owner-founder. Regardless of his competence as a professional manager, the president sometimes finds himself in a situation where
his competence will be criticized by those people resisting change.

REALIZED POWER

Realized power is the actual power gained by the president during his
tenure. Where the potential power is in the no-win range, the president's

realized power will be too low to enable him to act effectively, regardless of his personal characteristics. Where the potential power falls in the possible-win range, the president's characteristics determine how much of the potential power is converted to realized power.

At Design Associates, the potential power from coalition with the board was in the no-win range. The board is composed entirely of the firm's executives and lacks the power, because of its composition as well as the owner-founders' ownership position, to countermand the owner-founders. The potential power from coalition with the owner-founders was also in the no-win range. Lastly, since the firm has no outside investors or outstanding loans, there was no possibility for a coalition with these parties. Thus the potential power of any person appointed as president was in the no-win range. Cooper's low realized power was further assured by what the executives assessed as his inability to assume the role of the president of a small industrial design firm and to build effective personal relationships. The transition at Design Associates is diagrammed in Table 6, part A.

At both Home Mortgages and Control Systems, the potential power was greater than at Design Associates. At the former companies, the potential power fell within the possible-win range. At Home Mortgages, the amount of potential power from coalition with Samuels was questionable. The board members as well as the executives disagreed about Samuels' willingness to support any president, one group believing that the potential power was in the no-win range and the other opposing this contention. The potential power from coalition with the board was definitely in the possible-win range. The outside board members would have supported a president whom they believed to be competent because of their concern about transition from management by Samuels and his family to professional management and because of Samuels' age. The potential power from coalition with outside financial supporters was also in the possible-win range. Home Mortgages' need for loans, along with the fact that it had experienced severe financial crises, made it especially dependent on its lenders. The lenders shared the board's conviction that a professional president must be introduced into the firm. The sum of these sources of potential power for the new president was in the possible-win range.

Samuels and Madanick were not able to build a stable working relationship with each other. After a year of Madanick's presidency, the two men were headed on a collision course. Each realized that he needed the board's support to defeat the other man. The board first attempted to mediate between the two executives but recognized the futility of this course of action when Samuels asked Madanick for his resignation. The board was now in the position of having to choose between the two men. The outside board members conferred with a top executive to assess Madanick's competence. This executive confirmed the assessment of three of the outside board

TABLE 6

Conceptual Framework Applied to Sites

A. DESIGN ASSOCIATES

Potential power from coalition with owner-founder:
no-win range

Potential power from coalition with board:
no-win range

Potential power from coalition with
outside financial supporters: no-win range

Potential power:
no-win range

Personal characteristics
of president: inadequate

Realized power: LOW

B. HOME MORTGAGES COMPANY

Potential power from coalition with owner-founder:
questionable

Potential power from coalition with board:
possible-win range

Potential power from coalition with outside
financial supporters: possible-win range

Potential power:
possible-win range

Personal characteristics
of president: undetermined

Realized power: LOW

C. CONTROL SYSTEMS INC.

Potential power from coalition with owner-founder:
questionable

Potential power from coalition with board:
possible-win range

Potential power from coalition with outside
financial supporters: possible-win range

Potential power:
possible-win range

Personal characteristics
of president: superior

Realized power: HIGH

D. METAL MANUFACTURING COMPANY

Potential power from coalition with owner-founder:
possible-win range

Potential power from coalition with board:
possible-win range

Potential power from coalition with outside
financial supporters: possible-win range

Potential power:
possible-win range

Personal characteristics
of president: superior

Realized power: HIGH

Source: Compiled by the author.

95

members that Madanick was not sufficiently competent as president. The board then decided to support Samuels' request to ask for Madanick's resignation. The evaluation of Madanick's personal characteristics in his role as president is classified as undetermined: although the board members felt he had not fulfilled their expectations, approximately half of the executives questioned judged his abilities as adequate. The transition at Home Mortgages is diagrammed in part B of Table 6.

At Control Systems, the sum of the potential power available to the president from the three sources of power was in the possible-win range. The potential power from coalition with the owner-founder was questionable. Kelly, the owner-founder, stated that he wanted a successor in the long run. On the other hand, according to others interviewed, he had acted to reduce Davis' power and authority while Davis was the executive vice president. However, coalition with the board was a strong source of potential power for the president. The board was more powerful than Kelly, since it was composed of venture capitalists whose firms owned 75 percent of Control Systems' stock. In addition, the board wanted to replace Kelly with a new president because of its growing mistrust of Kelly and disagreements with him. As the company had made high loan demands, its banks were in a position to influence the owner-founder and the board. They were not involved in the decision to appoint a new president because the company was performing well financially. But, as they had no close relationship with Kelly and did not consider him irreplaceable, they had no objections to the new president. Hence, the potential power from coalition with outside financial supporters was in the possible-win range.

Kelly was aware of the coalition between Davis and the board. When he was appointed chairman, he realized that his position might be a temporary one. According to the firm's executives, during the time when Kelly was chairman, he concentrated his efforts on obtaining a larger equity position in the firm and on increasing the liquidity of his stocks. One executive stated:

> Kelly asked my secretary that a copy of the forecast be sent to his home, and she sent it.... When I found out, I told her to stop sending it. Next month, when he asked her for it, she told him to come to see me. He came to see me, and I said I had discussed this with Pete Davis, and we decided he should not have access to it. He said, "okay," and left. He didn't make a fuss. If he had made a fuss, he knew he wouldn't have gotten anywhere. He was shut down.

A few months after his appointment as chairman of the board, the board dissolved the position of chairman. This was a unanimous decision by the other board members, based on what they considered possibly unethical activities on Kelly's part. The decision was facilitated by the facts that

Kelly's expertise was replaceable and a competent president was already managing the firm. The situation at Control Systems Inc. can be delineated as shown in part C of Table 6.

At Metal Manufacturing, the potential power available to the new president was greater than at any of the other sites. Ryan had assumed most of the president's responsibilities for several years prior to his appointment as president. Both Thomas Gregg, the owner-founder, and the board considered Ryan's performance in this capacity to be excellent. By the time of the new president's appointment, the position of the president as separate from that of the owner-founder had already been established, and Gregg was accustomed to delegating the daily operations to another man. Consequently, the potential power from coalition with the owner-founder was in the possible-win range. The board was concerned with succession from the owner-founder to a professional manager and had observed the successful performance of a professional manager at Metal Manufacturing. Thus the potential power from coalition with board members was also in the possible-win range. The potential power from outside financial supporters was in the possible-win range for the same reasons as at Control Systems. At Metal Manufacturing, Ryan's extreme competence as president served to convert most of the potential power to realized power. There was no question in the executives' minds as to who evaluated them, who rewarded them, and who made the decisions regarding the firm's daily operations. The transition at Metal Manufacturing Company is diagrammed in part D of Table 6.

This chapter has presented a conceptual framework that emphasizes the existence of fundamental psychological and organizational forces which, in some situations, predetermine the fate of whomever is appointed president. The framework provides a language for describing and analyzing the final outcome of the transition from the owner-founder to a professional president in a given company.

NOTES

1. This corroborates Emerson's definition of power. He defines power of actor A over actor B as equal to the dependence of B upon A. The more the owner-founder is dependent upon the president, the more power the president has vis-à-vis the owner-founder, and so the more likely the owner-founder is to form a coalition with the president to improve his power in relation to the president.

2. Theodore Caplow, *Two Against One: Coalitions in Triads* (Englewood Cliffs, N.J.: Prentice-Hall, 1968).

3. John J. Gabarro, "The New General Manager and the Development of Trust, Influence and Expectations" (working paper, Harvard University, Graduate School of Business Administration, February 1976); quoted with special permission of the author.

4. Richard C. Hodgson, Daniel J. Levinson, and Abraham Zaleznik, *The Executive Role Constellation: An Analysis of Personality and Role Relations in Management* (Boston: Division of Research, Harvard University, Graduate School of Business Administration, 1965), p. 247.

6

IMPLICATIONS FOR MANAGERS AND RESEARCHERS

The purpose of the work reported in this book is to improve management of the transition from owner-founder to professional president by increasing management's understanding of this process. The first part of this chapter draws on the findings presented in the preceding chapters to make recommendations regarding better management of the process. Recommendations will be presented separately to the different parties—the owner-founders, the board of directors, the presidents, and the executives—because of the divergence in objectives and roles of each group. This does not, however, preclude some recommendations made to one group from being applicable to another group.

Although this study has focused on the transition from owner-founder to a person not his relative, many of the findings and recommendations are also applicable to situations where the new president is a relative of the owner-founder. The owner-founder's resistance to changing his style of management was also observed by Hershon in his study of management succession in family businesses. In the majority of the companies he studied, there was no change in the style used to manage the firm during the owner-founder's management of the firm. The change in management style took place only when the second generation had taken over the firm's management responsibilities.[1] Furthermore, Hershon, Levinson, and Davis observed the owner-founder's resistance to delegating to the relative who had replaced him as president.[2] The similarities in these findings suggest that the recommendations in this chapter may also be useful to organizations where a relative replaces the owner-founder as president.

RECOMMENDATIONS TO OWNER-FOUNDERS

Early in the firm's history, the owner-founder should make a conscious decision regarding the amount of control he wishes to maintain over the firm's management. Ideally, this factor should be taken into consideration in choosing the industry in which to establish a business. In cases where the company is already established, the owner-founder's decision regarding his desired level of control over the company should influence the company's strategy regarding growth in management complexity—be it through increase in sales volume, number of products, channels of distribution, or other actions.[3]

Determining the Company's Strategy
As Regards Management Complexity

The owner-founder's control of the company's management can be reduced in two ways: through expanding dependence on external financing and through greater dependence on other individuals to manage the company. As the organization's management becomes more and more complex, both these dependencies tend to increase, the result being decreased control by the owner-founder.

As the company grows in volume, even if all other components determining its complexity remain constant, its financing needs, be they for investment in the buildings and machinery or for working capital, also increase. Consequently, at a point determined by the enterprise's profitability and rate of growth, the financial needs of the company will surpass the internally generated funds, and outside financing will be required. Outside financing usually causes a reduction in the owner-founder's control over the firm. When venture capital investors provide financing, they usually require a seat on the board as well as adherence to various stipulations regarding the company's operations and personnel as a condition for contribution of equity. The banks may also make stipulations regarding the company's operations, in the form of financial conditions and employment of key personnel, before agreeing to a loan. The source of outside financing with least restrictions is sale of stock to the public at large if such a market exists. Given a widespread dispersion of stock, the major requirement of these public stockholders is increase in the market price of the stocks and/or dividends. As compared to loans, however, the sale of the firm's stock has the disadvantage of reducing the owner-founder's ownership position. Regardless of the form of outside financing, greater dependence on such financing reduces the owner-founder's control of the company.

Complexity of management also reduces the owner-founder's control over the organization by augmenting his reliance on other managers. As the firm grows in complexity, the owner-founder has less and less time for the decisions and actions necessary for the company's success and is therefore compelled to rely on the firm's executives in managing the firm.

If the owner-founder has a choice of industries in which to start a business, he should, in making this choice, take into account his desire for control. The owner-founder who desires a high degree of control should choose an industry with low capital requirements, so as to reduce reliance on outside financing. Secondly, he should choose industries that are less influenced by economies of scale and do not require a fast growth rate to remain competitive. Finally, he is well advised to avoid industries in which rapid technological change is likely to render his own knowledge and skills obsolete.

The owner-founder may be influenced by personal and economic factors in deciding on the company's strategy with regard to increasing management complexity. The personal considerations that sway many owner-founders toward higher complexity are: the sense of personal accomplishment brought on by the firm's growth; an insatiable desire for further achievement; and possible expansion of personal wealth. The economic factors that encourage greater complexity are: the importance of economies of scale in maintaining competitive costs; customers' demands for a larger product line, stockholders' demands for growth in sales; and changes in technology.

Implications of Increasing Management Complexity

For all entrepreneurial owner-founders, growing complexity of the firm's management inevitably necessitates a transition to a professional style of management. Numerous authors have attested to the necessity of such a change.[4] Entrepreneurial owner-founders can deal with this requirement in four possible ways: by doing nothing; by changing their style of management to a more professional style; by bringing in a professional manager as president; and by disassociating themselves from the firm's management.

Some entrepreneurial owner-founders justify doing nothing in this regard by rationalizing the company's problems in terms of external factors, even though the causes lie in the owner-founder's entrepreneurial style of management. The lack of action is facilitated if the board has little power vis-à-vis the owner-founder or if it hesitates to initiate action leading to conflict with the owner-founder. This is the wrong path in the long run; the situation inevitably worsens to result in serious financial problems for the company and, indirectly, for the owner-founder as a major stockholder.

Changing his style of management to a more professional one is the second alternative for the entrepreneurial owner-founder. He is usually encouraged to do so by outside board members. Except for a few exceptional individuals, most entrepreneurial owner-founders do not or cannot sufficiently alter their management styles to permit the firm's success. Some of the owner-founder's reasons for not changing their styles of management are as follows: the belief that the entrepreneurial management style is not the cause of the company's problems; lack of professional management skills such as establishing and using formal control systems; the belief that changing the management style will hurt the firm; and the satisfaction derived from involvement in daily operations. Even if the entrepreneurial owner-founder is willing to adapt his management style, the process of change usually takes many years and is only feasible when the firm can afford to wait these years.

When the owner-founder will not or cannot professionalize his management style, often the only alternative is to appoint a professional president. In considering such an appointment, the owner-founder should *first* assess the amount of potential power from a coalition between the president and himself. This assessment requires the owner-founder to examine *candidly* his feelings towards being replaced, his willingness to relinquish authority, and his tolerance for other management styles. How willing is he to support a new president? In answering this question, the entrepreneurial owner-founder should bear in mind that the potential power available to a president from most entrepreneurial owner-founders is in the no-win range.

If the president's potential power from coalition with the owner-founder is in the no-win range, the president may be doomed to failure. Unless the owner-founder's attitude and actions change, any newly appointed president is doomed to failure. In such situations, many presidents may be hired and fired—resulting in a negative organizational and financial impact on the firm—while the problems arising from lack of similarity between the owner-founder's entrepreneurial management style and the firm's management requirements become more and more severe.

In situations where the entrepreneurial owner-founder does not sufficiently modify his style of management and at the same time undermines the succession to a professional president, the best alternative for the owner-founder is to sell his ownership of the firm, resign from any positions he may hold in the firm, and start a new firm or pursue other interests. If the owner-founder cannot sufficiently change his management style to fit the environment, he should change the environment to fit his style. In this way, the firm is saved from eventual demise, and the owner-founder's wealth is preserved. Zaleznik and Kets de Vries also recommend this course of action in *Power and the Corporate Mind:*

The entrepreneurial presonality is a study in contradictions: imaginativeness and rigidity, the urge to take risks and the stubborn resistance to change. People often speculate about the possibility of changing the personality characteristics of innovators to eliminate the destructive qualities while preserving, if not enhancing, the constructive tendencies. These speculations are often based on wishful thinking—to have the best of the two possible worlds of innovation and maturation. Greater self-awareness and discipline would undoubtedly serve innovators well in making the transition from leading a new organization to conducting its operation during later stages of growth. But it is the rare individual who can develop this kind of awareness. Perhaps the more intelligent plan for an entrepreneur is to move away from his old venture while moving towards other areas of innovation. Instead of trying to change himself, he can continue to be a pioneer, but on new frontiers.[5]

Choosing one of the above three alternatives—changing one's management style; giving up the president's post with its authority and responsibility; or disassociating oneself managerially from one's creation—is an emotionally difficult task for the owner-founder. Yet in most firms that are increasing in management complexity, the owner-founder must candidly examine his own motivations and objectives and choose the alternative which best meets the goals of being emotionally least difficult and financially most rewarding for himself and the firm.

Providing for a Smooth Succession

The above recommendations are addressed to owner-founders of firms with a strategy of increasing management complexity. In firms where the decision is made to keep the management complexity at a low level, the replacement of the owner-founder can be delayed. Yet, even in these firms, the owner-founder should plan for succession in the case of his sudden incapacitation or his sudden death or his retirement. One step essential for a smooth succession is internal management development, so that a pool of competent candidates will be available to replace the owner-founder should the need arise. Secondly, the owner-founder should have the board members meet frequently with the executives so that the board will be able to make sound judgements of the executives' capabilities. In the case of retirement, the best option for most entrepreneurial owner-founders is to retire completely and sell their shares in the firm. Thus a new president will have the necessary authority and responsibility to manage the firm without the interference that often occurs when the entrepreneurial owner-founder remains associated with the firm.

If the owner-founder does remain associated with the firm after the president's appointment, he should (though we state this with some sense of futility) delegate authority commensurate with the president's responsibility to him. The owner-founder should divorce himself from daily operations and allow the president to manage the firm. This is particularly true in situations where the board has little power vis-à-vis the owner-founder. The more divergent the president's management style is from the owner-founder's, the more resistance the new president will be shown by the executives and, consequently, the more he will need the owner-founder's support in order to succeed. Unfortunately, situations where the president is most in need of support are those where he is least likely to gain support. This is a further reason for the recommendation that the owner-founder should resign from all his posts and truly retire from the firm as soon as the president is appointed.

In all cases, the owner-founder should establish a board of directors. A well-chosen board of directors can ensure the continued existence and success of the firm if the owner-founder becomes incapacitated or dies unexpectedly. For three reasons, the majority of the board members should be outsiders: If outsiders with expertise in general management or different management functions are appointed, the firm can use their expertise in improving its efficiency and effectiveness. The second advantage in having outside board members is that they tend to view the events and operations taking place in the firm more objectively than do directors who are also full-time employees of the firm. This advantage is particularly important in successions from the owner-founder to another person. The board's more objective viewpoint is a necessary balance to the owner-founder's emotional involvement. Even if the board does not have the power to take action counter to the owner-founder's desire, it can at least attempt to gain the owner-founder's support for the president by presenting him with the president's and their own views of the problems. Lastly, most of the advantages of having the firm's executives on the board can be realized by having these executives attend the appropriate board meetings, but without voting rights.

RECOMMENDATIONS TO BOARDS OF DIRECTORS

In their study, *The Board of Directors and Business Management,* Copeland and Towl state:

> The continuing existence of a corporate enterprise is one of the chief concerns of a board of directors. The board is the mechanism provided in corporate organizations for assuring the continuity of operations.[6]

Provision for a successful succession is a particularly significant responsibility of board members of firms managed by owner-founders, because in such firms there is usually no precedence or established mechanism for the replacement of the owner-founder. It is the board's duty not only to provide for the owner-founder's succession but to establish procedures for all future successions.

The successful replacement of the owner founder as president is an important task for the board members regardless of the firm's ownership structure. If the firm has stockholders other than the owner-founder, the board must obviously insure continued operation of the firm to protect those stockholders' interests. Even in firms where the owner-founder is the sole owner, the board still must insure the firm's survival because of its moral obligations to the firm's employees for their continued employment, to the creditors for repayment of their loans, and to society for the survival of an economic enterprise.

Succession is ordinarily necessitated either by the owner-founder's age or by the inappropriateness of his management style to the firm's needs. As suggested above, the board should question—rather than assume—the necessity of increased management complexity. In deciding the firm's strategy as to level of complexity, the board should consider the market and technology requirements as well as the stockholders' and owner-founder's needs. In cases of conflicting demands, the board must balance these demands in reaching a decision.

Whenever financial or operational problems arise in firms with entrepreneurial owner-founders, the board should determine whether the cause is the incongruency between the owner-founder's management style and the firm's management requirements. If the board identifies this to be the problem early enough, the firm will have the time to try several alternatives for dealing with the problem. The first alternative is to attempt to persuade the entrepreneurial owner-founder to adopt a more professional style of management. In some cases, moderate changes such as use of formal plans and budgeting are adequate to solve the firm's problem, and the owner-founder may be willing to adopt these innovations. In other cases, the source of the problem may be the owner-founder's failure to delegate sufficient responsibility to his managers. Persuading the owner-founder to alter his behavior in this regard will be a far more difficult task. Some owner-founders do succeed at it. However, if it should happen that the owner-founder will not or cannot modify his management style, the board may have no choice but to appoint a professional president to deal with the firm's problems.

Deciding to Appoint a President

Before considering whom to appoint, the board should *first* determine what the owner-founder's relationship will be with any person appointed president. When the president's potential power from coalition with the owner-founder is assessed to be in the no-win range, there will be problems in the relationship between the two men. In such cases, if the owner-founder's contributions to the firm's management can be replaced, the best alternative for the company may be to persuade the owner-founder to resign from his management or board positions. As Copeland and Towl suggest,

> If a board of directors decides to choose a new chief executive while "the old man" is still active, it is incumbent on the board to have a clear-cut understanding that "retirement" means "retirement." It is a wise executive who can really retire and avoid interference with his successor, and it is an unwise board of directors which permits a compromise on retirement.[7]

The present study reaffirms this recommendation not only for situations where the owner-founder is retiring, but for those where the president's potential power from coalition with the owner-founder is in the no-win range.

If the owner-founder insists on maintaining managerial association with the firm and the board does not have the power to oppose him, then the board should expect the president to fail. This failure will pose financial as well as organizational threats to the firm. A possible benefit from appointing a president in spite of the no-win situation is that the owner-founder may realize that no succession will be successful as long as he maintains a managerial association with the firm or adheres to a policy of nondelegation. But the probability of such a realization is low because many owner-founders explain such failures in nonpersonal terms, attributing them mainly to the president's lack of competence. As a result, in most no-win situations, appointing a president fails to address the firm's problems. In such situations, the board should delay the appointment, if possible, and focus their efforts on convincing the owner-founder to resign from his board and management positions.

Selecting a President

The board should consider the selection of an individual as president only *after* it has assessed the owner-founder's reaction to the president and taken whatever steps possible to improve the conditions for a successful changeover. Replacing an owner-founder is a very difficult task. Therefore, when choosing a successor to the owner-founder, board members should be demanding on the matter of the president's business and interpersonal competence.

The question always confronting the board in the appointment of a president is whether to promote an insider or hire an outsider. Promoting an insider is possible only if there are insiders who meet the competency requirements of the job. The advantages of promoting an insider are that he knows the firm's business and its norms and does not require the orientation time necessary for an outsider to learn about the firm; he also knows the employees and, especially, the owner-founder's personality and other characteristics. If used well, this knowledge may aid him in becoming accepted as president. Another benefit of appointing an insider is that the succession can take place in an evolutionary manner, as was done at Metal Manufacturing. The president-to-be can take on new responsibility as he becomes ready for it. This evolutionary method of succession is of course only possible if the owner-founder is willing to give up the responsibility and authority to the "heir apparent" or understudy.

There are several advantages to hiring an outsider. He has no prior allegiance or relationship with any group that could restrict his actions. This is particularly important when the owner-founder continues his association with the firm. In one firm, a board member made this statement:

> The owner and I both want an inside man to become president. But his reasons and mine differ. My reason is that I would know he can do the job. His reason is that he is comfortable with the guy and knows him and knows that, in a tight situation, he can sway him.

The second advantage of employing an outsider is that he is more likely than an insider to have a management style that is different from the owner-founder's. Longtime executives have a propensity to adopt the owner-founder's style of management. Hence, if the board aims to use the president as an agent for change, they should carefully consider the advantages of appointing an outsider. If on the other hand, the board desires existing management methods to continue, it would be well advised to appoint an insider. In all cases, the board should use the selection of the president to implement the firm's objectives. As Copeland and Towl state,

> Although the fact may not always be recognized by a board of directors, the selection of an executive and the making of policy are inseparable. By its choice of an executive, a board in effect determines whether old policies are to be followed or a new course charted. Hence, from this standpoint, too, its actions in filling an executive vacancy have long-range implications.[8]

Determining the Responsibilities of President and Owner-Founder

If the owner-founder does retain a management position in the company, the division of responsibility between the owner-founder and the president should be discussed in detail by the board members, the president-to-be, and the owner-founder before the president's appointment. Questions such as what the owner-founder's involvement in specific areas will be or what "consult with me regarding the major decisions" finally means, should be discussed. Through these discussions, the expected change in the owner-founder's role in the firm must be stressed to him. The more specific the discussions, the more information the board and the president will have in assessing the president's potential power from coalition with the owner-founder. Such discussions may convince the owner-founder that he will not enjoy his new role in the firm and that having no management position in the firm at all may be his best alternative.

It is important that the job titles of the owner-founder and the president reflect as clearly as possible the division of responsibility that has been decided, so as to reduce the chances for misunderstandings. Titles are also important since they provide the bearer with formal authority and act as a source of power for him. If the president's formal title does not equal his responsibilities, it is extremely easy for the owner-founder, who holds the title and therefore the formal authority, to reclaim responsibility for areas that were informally intended to be the president's.

The owner-founders who were studied all preferred to retain the title of chairman of the board as well as of chief executive officer. Even Thomas Gregg gave up the title of chief executive officer with some reluctance. For several reasons, it is advisable for the president to be the chief executive officer. First, since it is very difficult to delineate the division of responsibility between the chief executive officer and the chief operating officer, this method of dividing responsibility invites conflict between the president and the owner-founder. Secondly, when entrepreneurial owner-founders are chief executive officers, they often feel that the president does not have an authorized direct line of communication to the board. Rather, they see themselves as being the intermediary between the board and the president and as having authority and control over the flow of information and opinion between the board and the president. As a result, the board is less likely to be informed about the president's view of the transition process or the firm's operations and is likely to act on the basis of one viewpoint. Thirdly, by appointing the president as chief executive officer, the board makes his accountability to them much more clear-cut. He is totally responsible for the firm's operations within the guidelines set by the board. This accountability facilitates the evaluation of the president's performance.

All owner-founders at our sites assumed the position of chairman of the board upon the new president's appointment. This is a desirable position from the owner-founder's viewpoint because it allows him to maintain contact with the firm and gives him the authority to influence its overall direction. From the firm's viewpoint, the benefits are that the firm continues to utilize the owner-founder's experience and expertise. Futhermore, the owner-founder can act as a stabilizing influence during the initial period of the president's appointment, as was the case at Metal Manufacturing. However, these benefits to the firm are realized *only* in cases where the owner-founder is willing to delegate authority to the president. When the owner-founder acts to undermine the president, the harm done by the owner-founder's association outweighs the benefits.

Chairman of the board is not an appropriate position for most entrepreneurial owner-founders. The function of the chairman is to coordinate the board in establishing general policies and strategies and to insure their satisfactory implementation by the chief executive officer. This function is not congruent with the management style of entrepreneurial owner-founders. They do not see formulation of strategy as an important function but rather as a by-product of their operational decisions. The chairman of the board uses the firm's organization structure, measurement, information, and reward systems to insure the achievement of objectives. Rather than being concerned with the *process* of management, the entrepreneurial owner-founder is primarily concerned with the detail and substance of management. The chairman of the board is required to manage through other people. One of the predominant tendencies of the entrepreneurial owner-founder is his preference for personal involvement in operations over delegation of duties to other people. Lastly, according to Jaime Grego, one of the most important functions of the chairman of the board is to act as mediator.[9] The owner-founder's personal involvement in most conflicts and issues needing a mediator prevents him from having the objectivity necessary to perform the job.

The only other possible position for the owner-founder in the firm is to head an area and thus serve in a subordinate capacity to the new president. This might be a viable alternative for the owner-founder whose primary interest is research and who wishes to delegate the responsibility for the firm's management to others. For most owner-founders who are not research-oriented, staying in the firm in a subordinate position will lead to conflict with the president. The owner-founder continues to consider himself as chief executive even though he no longer holds this capacity. The president's deviation from paths that would have been taken by the owner-founder, were he still chief executive, leads to the owner-founder's undermining of the president. This scenario is corroborated by the experience of the venture capitalists interviewed. The lack of a viable position for the entrepreneurial owner-founder serves as a reason to encourage the owner-founder to disassociate himself managerially from the firm.

Board's Role after Appointment of President

Once the new president assumes his post, the board should make an effort to keep informed of the president's relationship with the owner-founder if the latter remains associated with the organization. The board's aim should be to provide a smooth transition by acting as mediator between the new president and the owner-founder. The board should attempt to reduce misunderstanding, act as a source of communications, and defuse potential conflict. Through persuasion or more direct use of power, the board should provide the requisite support for the president so that he can act as president.

If the disagreement between the president and the owner-founder becomes irreconcilable, the board should determine the cause of the conflict—to what extent is it due to the president's personal characteristics and to what extent to the owner-founder's attitude toward the president, regardless of the latter's attributes. This analysis should be used by the board to determine what actions should be taken to increase the chances of success for the next president. In some cases, where the problems are caused by the president's personal characteristics, it may be sufficient to replace him with another president. In other situations, the problems lie with the owner-founder's unwillingness to cooperate with any president. The best action here is for the owner-founder to resign from the firm's management. Finally, a third situation can exist where the owner-founder undermines the president, but the president is also less competent than desired. In such cases, the board can choose between two alternatives. It can comply with the owner-founder's wish and fire the president, under the condition that the owner-founder first agrees to changes that will enhance the next president's chance of success. Home Mortgages' board of directors attempted to use this strategy. The best agreement is to obtain the owner-founder's resignation in return for firing the president. If he does not agree to this, one compromise would be to have him agree to retire within a certain period of time or to allow the next president to be the chief executive officer. The second alternative is to fire the owner-founder in order to prevent a reversion to his management and to plan to later replace the president with a more competent person.

The above recommendations assume the board's power is great enough to overcome any resistance offered by the owner-founder. Usually, the implementation of actions that are met by the owner-founder's severe resistance requires the board, or at least the majority of its members, to be united in their support for the course of action. Consequently, such agreement should be reached before any action is taken, so as to assure the effective implementation of the chosen course of action.

RECOMMENDATIONS TO PRESIDENTS

When asked about how much of his experience as president he had anticipated, Bill Cooper said, "I know that neither the president nor the owner-founder has any idea of how delicate a situation it is before he gets into it." The concept of potential power provides the candidate for the president's position with a strong tool for determining whether he has any chance of success. This analysis should then be used to decide whether or not to accept the appointment.

Deciding to Accept the Position of President

Potential power from coalition with the owner-founder is determined by the factors delineated in Table 7. As a first step to determine the potential power from coalition with the owner-founder, the president should identify the owner-founder's management style. An insider may be able to make this determination from his knowledge of the situation. An outsider must obtain information through questioning executives, board members, and the owner-founder. In order to assure the validity of the information obtained, he should ask questions from a variety of executives and board members—for example, both inside board members and outsiders, new executives as well as "old timers." The president should ask questions about the type of decisions in which the owner-founder becomes directly involved. In particular: does he usually become involved in operations on a routine basis, or is the basis for his involvement the variance of performance from a set level? Questions should also be asked about the de facto structure of the organization and the methods used for planning, evaluation, and performance measurement.

If the owner-founder has an entrepreneurial style of management, there is a very high probability that the potential power from the owner-founder's coalition with the president will fall in the no-win range. The owner-founder will most likely not give the president the authority necessary to act as president and will make decisions that should be made by the president. This is what took place at all sites with an entrepreneurial owner-founder.

Even in cases where the owner-founder has a professional style of management, the potential power from coalition with him may still be in the no-win range because of his psychological attributes. One indication of the owner-founder's attitudes to succession is his past experience with an heir apparent, a number two man, or a past president. The failure of these individuals should strongly indicate potential problems. The second way of

TABLE 7
Factors Determining Potential Power

A. *From Coalition with Owner-Founder*
   Management style of the owner-founder
   Owner-founder's personal attributes
      Need for control
      Jealousy of president
      Fear of being displaced
   Dependence of the owner-founder on the president.

B. *From Coalition with Board of Directors*
   Board's power vis-à-vis owner-founder
      Control over firm's equity or loans
      Board's composition
         Number of inside members
         Number of outsiders who rely on owner-founder for income
         Emotional ties
      Importance and necessity of owner-founder's contributions

   If the board has sufficient power, the decision to form a coalition with the
   president depends on:
      Concern with a smooth succession
      Impact of owner-founder's departure on stockholders, customers, suppliers.

C. *From Coalition with Investors*
   Investors' power vis-à-vis owner-founder
      Control over firm's equity or liquidity
      Importance and necessity of owner-founder's contributions

   If the investors have sufficient power, the decision to form a coalition with the
   president depends on:
      Concern with smooth succession
      Impact of owner-founder's departure on other stockholders, customers, suppliers.

Source: Compiled by the author.

identifying the owner-founder's feelings about succession is through listening
for them in conversations with the owner-founder. Finally, examining the
owner-founder's role in the appointment process often reflects his attitudes to
a president. Did the owner-founder initiate the process? How supportive was
he about appointing a president? The greater the owner-founder's reluctance,
the greater the likelihood of a no-win situation. If the potential power from

coalition with the owner-founder is in the no-win range, the president must have the support of the board and/or investors to succeed in this capacity.

The potential power from coalition with the board and investors is delineated in parts B and C of Table 7. Information regarding these factors may be obtained from annual reports, conversations with executives, board members, investors, and the owner-founder.

In summary, before accepting an appointment to the position of president, the executive should assess the total potential power available to him. If the potential power from coalition with the owner-founder is in the no-win range, he should further consider the presidency only if he is willing to deal with an owner-founder who will attempt to undermine him. He should also evaluate the potential power from coalition with the board and investors. If that too is in the no-win range, the president is doomed to failure. He should only accept the position on the basis of its economic rewards. In such cases, he should obtain an employment contract to increase the probability of realizing such rewards.

Actions as President

In companies where the owner-founder retains a position in management and where he has greater power than the board, obtaining the owner-founder's cooperation and support is vital to the president's survival. Even in possible-win situations, this is still a very difficult task because of the inherent contradictions in the relationship between many owner-founders and the presidents. The president's task is to obtain the owner-founder's support while wresting authority away from him, a seeming paradox. One way to deal with this paradox is through consultation with the owner-founder on major decisions. Thus, the president can obtain authority as well as the owner-founder's support. It will also allow the president to benefit from the owner-founder's experience and expertise. Furthermore, through such involvement, the president will know which actions will be resisted so strongly thay they are not feasible. He may have to compromise on some actions, but by involving the owner-founder in the decision making, the president will obtain his commitment for implementation of the actions that have been agreed upon. However, the extent of the president's consultation with the owner-founder is a very delicate issue that requires the balancing of contradictory demands made by the owner-founder. On the one hand, the latter wishes the president to closely follow his management style and implement his version of the firm's objectives. Yet, if the president acts in this manner, the owner-founder may criticize him for indecisiveness or weakness. The following statement by an owner-founder is an illustration of these contradictory demands:

One man can't be brought in and the other, me, put on top, saying, "Go ahead and do it." I suspect that he can, but he will be running his own firm rather than my firm.... Too often, a situation is one where you have to say, "Come on! Let's get up and do it!" [The president] does not have the perception and insight to say, "Here is what needs to be done and what we should do." Rather, he wants to be told what to do.

The president should always attempt to view his own actions from the viewpoint of the owner-founder, in light of the owner-founder's feeling, expectations, and management style. This may prevent him from taking some actions he had planned. In many cases, however, the president may not have to compromise on the ends, but rather on the means. Presenting change as a step that is building on the owner-founder's accomplishments will help to gain the owner-founder's support of the president. Presenting change in a way that implies the rejection or degradation of the owner-founder's efforts will result in the owner-founder's hostility to the president.

Support of the president by board members is vital to the president's survival if the owner-founder opposes the president. One way of gaining the board's support is through the use of formal means such as board meetings to present the firm's progress and thus show one's accomplishments. If the owner-founder is associated with the firm, the accomplishments should be presented as additions to the crucial accomplishments of the owner-founder who built the firm. The alert board members will not see this as a diminution of the president's own efforts, but rather as an illustration of his interpersonal skills. The president should also identify the most powerful board members and obtain their support through more informal means such as luncheons or other social interactions. When appropriate, the president should signal to the board members that their status in, and relationship with, the firm will remain unchanged with him as president, regardless of the owner-founder's association with the firm.

In some firms, the conflict between the president and the owner-founder makes the continued association of both persons with the firm impossible. When the board has the power to choose who will remain, the president must attempt to convince them that it is in the firm's best interest to have him remain as president. Four arguments may be used toward this end. First, the president should point to the firm's progress during his tenure as evidence of his beneficial impact on the firm. Secondly, if the owner-founder cannot, due to psychological reasons, support *any* president, this fact can be pointed out to the board by using the concept of potential power. If the board becomes convinced that the owner-founder will undermine any president, they will realize that the owner-founder's resignation from all posts in the firm is a prerequisite for an effective succession. Thirdly, the president should impress upon the board the negative impact of his dismissal on the next president's ability to gain cooperation and support from the executives. "The sharks have smelled blood" was the comment made by one manager regarding the firm's executives when realized that the president had been asked to resign. The fourth argument that the president may be able to use is that firing the president symbolizes reversion to management by the owner-founder and results in low morale for many executives. For example, after the president's dismissal, an executive of one firm said,"This kind of thing affects the enthusiasm of the people. We felt we were going some place and had done well. Now, the family is in control again."

RECOMMENDATIONS TO EXECUTIVES

In firms where an entrepreneurial owner-founder retains a management post after the president's appointment, the executives often perceive the relationship between the owner-founder and the president as being antagonistic. As a result, they often see themselves confronted with "taking sides" with the owner-founder or the president. Executives have two strategies for dealing with this issue.

The first strategy is to take the side of one party. If the party whom the executive supports becomes or stays the most powerful one, he will reward the executive for his support. For example, if the president becomes more powerful than the owner-founder, he will probably promote and amply reward those who supported him. However, there are several drawbacks to this strategy. If the executive supports the party who is fired or otherwise stripped of his power, the party whom he did not support may take retaliatory action against him. Therefore, the executive should carefully analyze the situation to determine who has a higher chance of winning. Those executives with long tenure in the company are especially prone to misjudge who is the stronger party through their tendency to see the owner-founder's power as equal to what it was in the firm's early years. The second disadvantage is that the board may look critically on executives who take sides by perceiving their action as hampering a smooth transition.

The second alternative is not to take sides and to try to stay impartial. The advantage of this course of action is that there is no risk of choosing the wrong side to support. Also, not getting involved in "politics" may be viewed as a positive attribute by the board, the president, or the owner-founder. The disadvantage is that the executive will not benefit from the rewards given to the supporters of the party that becomes most powerful.

The above two approaches are extreme solutions. In reality, it is difficult to find executives who exclusively practice either extreme. Yet, consideration of the benefits and concomitant weaknesses of each approach should help the executive balance the trade-offs and formulate the approach most suitable to his needs. At some sites, supporting one party may be the best alternative for the executive. This may be the case, for example, at sites where the owner-founder controls the firm's ownership and has little need of external financing and the board has little power. In the case of a conflict with the president, the owner-founder will undoubtedly be the winner.

At some firms, it may be advisable to support the president. This is the case in firms where the owner-founder himself supports the president, as at Metal Manufacturing, or in firms where the owner-founder leaves. In these situations, the executive should adapt his style to the president's management style or he should leave. The executive should examine his skills and flexibility and assess whether he will be able to adapt. If he decides that he will not be able to adapt, he should seek employment at a company where his management style and skills will fit the company's management requirements. He should take the initiative to change jobs before he is asked to resign. By taking the initiative, he will have more time to search and will also be more marketable because of his voluntary departure. The approach of remaining with the firm and attempting to resist change or undermine the president may lead to being fired by the president.

FUTURE RESEARCH

The suggestions for future research fall into two categories. The first is research directly related to this study. The second category is the study of other management problems related to the management problems discussed in this report.

Since this study was conducted at U.S. companies, the question can be raised of the applicability of its findings to firms in other cultures or countries. Studies similar to this one could be conducted in other cultures to test the universality of the findings reported here. What cultural differences are there in the owner-founder's psychological reaction to being replaced by a professional manager? What is the impact of the extended family system on the process? What is the impact of the differences in the board's role in different countries? What is the impact of different ways of handling conflict in different cultures?

Another course for future research is to select a more narrow research problem and use a larger number of sites to study it in greater depth. For example, any one of the phases of the transition—be it the process leading to the appointment of the president, the development of relationships in the first three months, or the process leading to the dismissal of either the president or the owner-founder—could be chosen for study in more depth.

An interesting study would be to test the predictive abilities of the power framework put forth in Chapter 5. The study could identify firms that are in the process of appointing a president but that have not yet made the final selection. By using the concept of potential power, the researcher could make an a priori prediction of the president's chances of success on the basis of the owner-founder's psychology and management style and the board's power. The researcher could then compare the final outcome with his predictions.

There are many other related management areas in which research could be instrumental in improving management practice. There are several ways of professionalizing the firm's management. The replacement of the owner-founder by a professional president is the alternative that was chosen for this study. Another method of professionalization of management is to bring in professional managers to supplement the owner-founder who remains as president. A third method involves the aquisition of entrepreneurially managed firms by larger firms. Customarily, such aquisitions stipulate the continued employment of the owner-founder for a certain number of years after the acquisition. The findings of this study imply that the latter situation would lead to severe conflicts between the entrepreneurial owner-founder and the firm's new owners. Nonetheless, a study of any of these alternative paths of professionalization of management would be interesting to the researcher as well as useful to management.

In being concerned with another facet, the present study has addressed the division of responsibility between the two top managers in the company. A study could be performed about the division of responsibility between chief executive officer and chief operating officer, or the president and the executive vice president(s), or the president and the chairman of the board. The following question could be asked about any of the relationships chosen for study: What is the formal versus informal division of responsibility? What factors determine the informal division of responsibility? What are the characteristics of the most effective division of responsibility?

The purpose of this study has been to improve the management of one of the difficult transitions confronting most firms at one point in their history. The preceding chapters described the transition from owner-founder to professional president and presented a framework for predicting and analyzing its final outcome. This closing chapter has presented recommendations for better management of the transition. It is hoped that this study as well as the future studies outlined above will be instrumental in improving what is still the "art" of management.

NOTES

1. Simon A. Hershon, "The Problems of Management Succession in Family Businesses" (D.B.A. dissertation, Harvard University, Graduate School of Business Administration, 1976), chap. 5.

2. Ibid.; Levinson, "Conflicts That Plague Family Businesses," *Harvard Business Review*

(March-April 1971): 90–98; Stanley M. Davis, "Entrepreneurial Succession," *Administrative Science Quarterly* (December 1968): 402–16.

3. For definition of complexity, see Chapter 1, pp. 8–10.

4. See Chapter 2, pp. 25–26.

5. Abraham Zaleznik and Manfred F.R. Kets de Vries, *Power and the Corporate Mind* (Boston: Houghton Mifflin, 1975), pp. 228–29.

6. Melvin T. Copeland and Andrew R. Towl, *The Board of Directors and Business Management* (Boston: Division of Research, Harvard University, Graduate School of Business Administration, 1947), p. 18.

7. Ibid., p. 36.

8. Ibid., p. 31.

9. Jaime Grego, "The Changing Role and Function of the Board of Directors" (D.B.A. dissertation, Harvard University, Graduate School of Business Administration, 1976), pp. 170–77.

BIBLIOGRAPHY

Books

Abegglen, James C., and W. Lloyd Warner. *Big Business Leaders in America.* New York: Harper & Brothers, 1955.

Argyris, Chris. *Increasing Leadership Effectiveness.* New York: John Wiley & Sons, 1976.

Barnard, Chester I. *The Functions of the Executive.* Cambridge: Harvard University Press, 1938.

Baty, Gordon C. *Entrepreneurship: Playing to Win.* Reston, Virginia: Reston, 1974.

Bell, David V.J. *Power, Influence, and Authority.* New York: Oxford University Press, 1975.

Boswell, Jonathon. *The Rise and Decline of Small Firms.* London, England: George Allen & Unwin, 1972.

Buchele, Robert B. *Business Policy in Growing Firms.* San Francisco: Chandler, 1967.

Caplow, Theodore. *Two Against One: Coalitions in Triads.* Englewood Cliffs, N.J.: Prentice-Hall, 1968.

Chandler, Alfred D., Jr. *Strategy and Structure.* Cambridge: MIT Press, 1962.

Christensen, C. Roland. *Management Succession in Small and Growing Enterprises.* Boston: Division of Research, Harvard University, Graduate School of Business Administration, 1953.

Coffey, Robert E., Anthony G. Athos, and Peter A. Reynolds, *Behavior in Organizations.* Englewood Cliffs, N.J.: Prentice-Hall, 1975.

Cohn, Theodore, and Roy A. Lindberg. *Survival and Growth: Management Strategies for the Small Firm.* New York: AMACOM, 1974.

Collins, Orvis, and David G. Moore. *The Organization Makers* New York: Appleton-Century Crofts, 1970.

Copeland, Melvin T., and Andrew R. Towl. *The Board of Directors and Business Management.* Boston: Division of Research, Harvard University, Graduate School of Business Administration, 1947.

Crozier, Michel. *The Bureaucratic Phenomenon.* Chicago: University of Chicago Press, 1964.

Cyert, Richard M., and James G. March. *A Behavioral Theory of the Firm*. Englewood Cliffs N.J.: Prentice-Hall, 1963.

Drucker, Peter. *The Practice of Management*. New York: Harper & Row, 1954.

Fortune Editors. *The Executive Life*. Garden City, N.Y.: Doubleday, 1956.

French, John R.P., and Bertram Raven. "The Bases of Social Power." In *Studies in Social Power*, edited by Dorwin Cartwright. Ann Arbor: University of Michigan Press, 1959.

Freud, Sigmund. "Mourning and Melancholia." In *Collected Papers*. Translated under supervision of Jan Rievieve. New York: Basic Books, 1959.

Galbraith, John Kenneth. *The New Industrial State*. Boston: Houghton Mifflin, 1971.

Glaser, Barney G., and Anselm L. Strauss. *The Discovery of Grounded Theory: Strategies for Qualitative Research*. Chicago, Illinois: Aldine, 1968.

Glickman, Albert S. Clifford P. Hahn, Edwin A. Fleishman, and Brent Baxter. *Top Management Development and Succession*. New York: Macmillan, 1968.

Gouldner, Alvin. *Patterns of Industrial Bureaucracy*. Glencoe, Ill.: Free Press, 1954.

Hodgson, Richard C., Daniel J. Levinson, and Abraham Zaleznik. *The Executive Role Constellation: An Analysis of Personality and Role Relations in Management*. Boston: Division of Research, Harvard University, Graduate School of Business Administration, 1965.

Homans, George C. *The Human Group*. New York: Harcourt, Brace, 1950.

Ianni, Francis A. J., and Elizabeth Reuss-Janni. *A Family Business*. New York: Russell Sage Foundation, 1972.

Jardim, Anne. *The First Henry Ford: A Study in Personality and Business Leadership*. Cambridge: MIT Press, 1970.

Klein, Howard J. *Stop! You're Killing the Business*. New York: Mason & Lipscomb, 1975.

Krentzman, Harvey C. *Managing for Profits*. Washington, D.C.: Government Printing Office for Small Business Administration, 1968.

Kübler-Ross, Elisabeth. *On Death and Dying*. New York: Macmillan, 1969.

Lenski, Gerhard E. *Power and Privilege: A Theory of Social Stratification*. New York: McGraw-Hill, 1966.

Lorsch, Jay William, and John J. Morse. *Organizations and Their Members: A Contingency Approach*. New York: Harper & Row, 1974.

McClelland. David C. *Power, The Inner Crisis*. New York: Irvington, 1975.

_____. *The Achieving Society*. New York: Free Press, 1961.

McClelland, David C., and David G. Winter. *Motivating Economic Achievement.* New York: Free Press, 1969.

Mace, Myles L. *The Board of Directors in Small Corporations.* Boston: Division of Research, Harvard University, Graduate School of Business Administration, 1948.

_____. *Directors, Myth and Reality.* Boston: Division of Research, Harvard University, Graduate School of Business Administration, 1971.

McGuire, Joseph W. *Factors Affecting the Growth of Manufacturing Firms.* Seattle: Bureau of Business Research, University of Washington Press, 1963.

Marcus, Stanley. *Minding the Store.* Boston: Little, Brown, 1974.

Martin, Norman H., and W. Lloyd Warner, eds. *Industrial Man.* New York: Harper & Brothers, 1959.

Neustadt, Richard E. *Presidential Power, The Politics of Leadership.* New York: John Wiley & Sons, 1960.

Pettigrew, Andrew M. *The Politics of Organizational Decision-Making.* London, England: Tavistock, 1975.

Rubel, Stanley M., and Edward G. Novotny, eds. *How to Raise and Invest Venture Capital.* New York: Presidents Publishing House, 1971.

Schachter, Stanley. *The Psychology of Affiliation.* Stanford: Stanford University Press, 1959.

Sofer, Cyril. *Organizations in Theory and Practice.* New York: Basic Books, 1972.

Thibaut, S., and H. H. Kelly. *The Social Psychology of Groups.* New York: John Wiley & Sons, 1959.

Thompson, James D. *Organizations in Action.* New York: McGraw-Hill, 1967.

Wilkie, Roy, and James N. Young. *The Owner-Managers and Managers of Small Firms: A Study in Depth.* Strathclyde, Scotland: University of Strathclyde, 1971.

Wolman, Benjamin B. *Victims of Success.* New York: Quadrangle, 1973.

Zaleznik, Abraham, and Manfred F. R. Kets de Vries. Power and the Corporate Mind. Boston: Houghton Mifflin, 1975.

Articles

Argyris, Chris. "The Chief Executive's Behavior: Key to Organizational Development." *Harvard Business Review* (March-April 1973): 55–64.

Ball, Robert. "Antoine Riboud's Own French Revolution." *Fortune* (September 1973): 216–22.

"Behind the Purge at CBS." *Time*, October 25, 1976, pp. 56–57.

Burck, Charles G. "How the Tisches Run Their 'Little Store.' " *Fortune* (May 1971): 158–61, 208–16.

_____. "Optel's (Mis)Adventures in Liquid Crystals." *Fortune* (October 1973): 192–96, 201–02.

Calder, Grant H. "The Peculiar Problems of A Family Business." *Business Horizons* (Fall 1961): 93–102.

Cambreleng, Robert W. "The Case of the Nettlesome Nepot." *Harvard Business Review* (March-April 1969): 14–22.

Carruth, Eleanore. "Genesco Comes to Judgement." *Fortune* (July 1975): 108–13.

_____. "The Growth-Producing Fission at Unionamerica." *Fortune* (March 1974): 122–25, 180–88.

_____. "Sweat + Leverage = $200 Million for Arthur Cohen." *Fortune* (December 1972): 133–41.

Clifford, Donald K. "The Case of the Floundering Founder." *Organizational Dynamics (Autumn 1975): 21–33.*

_____. "Growth Pains of the Threshold Company." *Harvard Business Review* (September-October 1973): 143–54.

Cordtz, Dan. "Bechtel Thrives on Billion Dollar Jobs." *Fortune* (January 1975): 91–93, 142–53.

Dahl, R. A. "The Concept of Power." *Behavioral Science* 2(1951): 201–15.

Davis, Stanley M. "Entrepreneurial Succession." *Administrative Science Quarterly* (December 1968): 402–16.

Donnelly, Robert G. "The Family Business." *Harvard Business Review* (July-August 1964): 93–105.

Emerson, Richard M. "Power Dependence Relations." *American Sociological Review* (February 1962): 31–41.

Ewing, David W. "Is Nepotism So Bad?" *Harvard Business Review* (January-February 1965): 223–36.

Golde, Roger A. "Practical Planning for Small Business." *Harvard Business Review* (September-October 1964): 147–63.

Greiner, Larry E. "Evolution and Revolution as Organizations Grow." *Harvard Business Review* (July-August 1972): 37–46.

Hickson, D. J., C. B. Hinnings, C. A. Lee, R. E. Schneck, and J. M. Pennings. "A Strategic Contingencies Theory of Intra-Organizational Power." *Administrative Science Quarterly* 2 (June 1971): 216–29.

Krentzman, Harvey C., and John N. Samaras. "Can Small Business Use Consultants?" *Harvard Business Review* (May-June 1960): 126–36.

Kulkosky, Edward. "CBS: The Agony and the Executives." *Financial World,* November 15, 1976, pp. 9–12.

Lenzner, Robert. "Land: The Man Behind the Camera." Boston *Globe,* October 17, 1976, p. Bl.

Levinson, Harry. "Don't Choose Your Own Successor." *Harvard Business Review* (November-December 1974): 53–62.

_____. "Conflicts That Plague Family Businesses." *Harvard Business Review* (March-April 1971): 90–98.

_____. "On Being a Middle-Aged Manager." *Harvard Business Review* (July-August 1969): 51–60.

Lippit, Gordon L., and Warren H. Schmidt. "Crises in a Developing Organization." *Harvard Business Review* (November-December 1967): 102–12.

Loving, Rusch, Jr. "Bob Six's Long Search for a Successor." *Fortune* (June 1975): 92–97, 175–78.

McClelland, David C. "Achievement Motivation Can Be Developed." *Harvard Business Review* (November-December 1965): 6–24.

McClelland, David C., and David H. Burnham. "Power is the Great Motivator." *Harvard Business Review* (March-April 1976): 100–10.

Mechanic, David. "Sources of Power of Lower Participants in Complex Organizations." *American Science Quarterly* 3 (December 1962): 349–64.

Newman, Louis E. "Advice for Small Company Presidents." *Harvard Business Review* (November-December 1959): 69–76.

Schrage, Harry. "The R & D Entrepreneur: Profile in Success." *Harvard Business Review* (November-December 1965): 56–69.

Schwartz, Edward L. "Will Your Business Die With You?" *Harvard Business Review* (September-October 1954): 110–21.

Scott, Bruce R. "The Industrial State: Old Myths and New Realities." *Harvard Business Review* (March-April 1973): 133–48.

Shaw, Robert. "What About Family-Owned Corporations that Have 'Gone Public'?" *The Magazine of Wall Street*, January 17, 1959, p. 411.

Steinmetz, Lawrence L. "Critical Stages of Small Business Growth." *Business Horizons*, February 12, 1969, pp. 29–36.

Strauss, George. "Adolescence in Organizational Growth: Problems, Pains, Possibilities." *Organizational Dynamics* (Spring 1974): 3–17.

Tilles, Seymour. "Survival Strategies for Family Firms." *European Business* (April 1970): 9–17.

Trow, Donald B. "Executive Succession in Small Companies." *Administrative Science Quarterly* (September 1961): 228–39.

White, L. T. "Management Assistance for Small Business." *Harvard Business Review* (July-August 1965): 67–74.

Young, Robert B. "Keys to Corporate Growth." *Harvard Business Review* (November-December 1961): 51–62.

Zaleznik, Abraham. "Power and Politics in Organizational Life." *Harvard Business Review* (May-June 1970): 47–60.

_____. "Management of Disappointment." *Harvard Business Review* (November-December 1967): 59–70.

_____. "The Human Dilemmas of Leadership." *Harvard Business Review* (July-August 1963): 49–56.

Legal Cases*

Barrett, Audrey, and Learned, E. P. "The Galvor Company." M. Armagnac, Technical Director. Boston, Massachusetts: Intercollegiate Case Clearing House, Part 1 #9-311-036, Part 2 #9-311-037, © 1965.

Boehlke, Robert J. "Vappi and Company, Inc." Boston, Massachusetts: Intercollegiate Case Clearing House, #6-371-296, © 1971.

Gearreald, Tull N. "Tensor Corporation." Boston, Massachusetts: Intercollegiate Case Clearing House, #9-370-041, © 1969.

Hower, Ralph, and Sheldon, Alan. "The Ford-Knudsen Case." Boston, Massachusetts: Intercollegiate Case Clearing House, #3-474-060, © n.d.

Laurin, Pierre. "General Automotive Supply (R)." Boston, Massachusetts: Intercollegiate Case Clearing House, #2-468-002, © 1967.

---

*Copyright © by the President and Fellows of Harvard College.

Leighton, C. M. "L. L. Bean Incorporated." Boston, Massachusetts: Intercollegiate Case Clearing House, #9-366-013, © 1965.

Scott, Bruce R. "The Stages of Corporate Development. Part I." Boston, Mass.: Intercollegiate Case Clearing House, # 9-371-294, © 1971.

_____. "Acoustic Research Inc. (A+B)." Boston, Massachusetts: Intercollegiate Case Clearing House, #6-312-020, #6-312-021, © 1959.

Sproat, Audrey T., and Christensen, C. Roland. "A Note on Corporate Board of Directors." Boston, Massachusetts: Intercollegiate Case Clearing House, #4-372-309, © 1972.

Stevenson, Howard H. "Head Ski Company, Inc." Boston, Massachusetts: Intercollegiate Case Clearing House, #6-313-120, © 1967.

Taguiri, Renato, and Leonhard, James. "President Elect." Boston, Massachusetts: Intercollegiate Case Clearing House, #9-474-195, © n.d.

Weigle, Charles B. "Dansk Design Limited." Boston, Massachusetts: Intercollegiate Case Clearing House, #6-371-288, © 1971.

No Authors Supplied

"Desert-Dry Rainwear Corporation." Boston, Massachusetts: Intercollegiate Case Clearing House, #4-676-011, © 1975.

"Mystic Electronics Company, Inc. (A+B)." Boston, Massachusetts: Intercollegiate Case Clearing House, #9-374-314, # 9-374-315, © 1974.

"Roberta Downing (A+B)1." Boston, Massachusetts: Intercollegiate Case Clearing House, #4-374-074, #4-374-075, © 1973.

"Terry Allen." Boston, Massachusetts: Intercollegiate Case Clearing House, #4-372-140, © 1971.

Dissertations

Grego, Jaime. "The Changing Role and Function of the Board of Directors." D.B.A. dissertation, Harvard University, Graduate School of Business Administration, 1976.

Hershon, Simon A. "The Problems of Management Succession in Family Businesses." D.B.A. dissertation, Harvard University, Graduate School of Business Administration, 1975.

Johnston, J. Russel. "An Analysis of Relationship of Individuals to a Rapidly Growing Organization." D.B.A. dissertation, Harvard University, Graduate School of Business Administration, 1971.

Kets de Vries, Manfred F. R. "The Entrepreneur as Catalyst of Economic and Cultural Change: A Psycho-Entrepreneurial Approach." D.B.A. dissertation, Harvard University Graduate School of Business Administration, 1970.

Prahalad, Coimbatore K. "The Strategic Process in Multinational Corporations." D.B.A. dissertation, Harvard University, Graduate School of Business Administration, 1975.

Salter, Malcolm S. "Stage of Corporate Development: Implications for Management Control." D.B.A. dissertation, Harvard University, Graduate School of Business Administration, 1968.

Unpublished Material

Gabarro, John J. "The New Manager and the Development of Trust, Influence, and Expectations." Working paper, Harvard University, Graduate School of Business Administration, February 1976. (Quoted with special permission from the author.)

Timmons, Jeffrey A. "The Entrepreneurial Team: Formation and Development." Paper, Northeastern University, Graduate School of Business Administration, June 1973.

Timmons, Jeffrey A. "The Entrepreneurial Team: An American Dream or Nightmare." Paper, Northeastern University, Graduate School of Business Administration, January 1975.

ABOUT THE AUTHOR

MARYAM TASHAKORI is assistant vice president of Construction Loan Division at the Riggs National Bank of Washington, D.C.

Dr. Tashakori holds an A.B. degree with distinction in all subjects from Cornell University and an M.B.A. and D.B.A. from the Graduate School of Business Administration at Harvard University. She is a member of Phi Beta Kappa, Phi Kappa Phi and Mortar Board.